STEPHEN MAXWELL was born in Edinburgh in 1942 to a Scottish medical family. He grew up in Yorkshire and was educated there before winning a scholarship to St John's College Cambridge, where he read Moral Sciences. This was followed by three years at the London School of Economics studying International Politics. Attracted by stirrings of Scottish Nationalism, he joined the London branch of the SNP in 1967. He worked as a research associate for the International Institute for Strategic Studies in London and a Lecturer in International Affairs at the University of Sussex. In 1970 he returned to Scotland as Chatham House Research Fellow at the University of Edinburgh. He was a frequent contributor to the cultural and political journals from *Scottish International Review* through *Question* to *Radical Scotland*, which fertilised the Scottish debate from the 1970s to the 1990s. From 1973 to 1978 he was the SNP's National Press Officer and was director of the SNP's 1979 campaign in the Scottish Assembly Referendum. He was an SNP councilor on Lothian Regional Council 1975–78 before serving as SNP Vice Chair, successively for Publicity, Policy and Local Government. From the mid-1980s, he worked in the voluntary sector, initially with Scottish Education and Action for Development (SEAD) and then for the Scottish Council for Voluntary Organisations (SCVO). He retired in 2009. He was the founding chair of a Scottish charitable company which today provides support to enable six hundred vulnerable people to live in the community. He contributed to numerous collections of essays on Scotland's future, most recently *The Modern SNP: from Protest to Power* (ed Hassan, EUP, 2009), *Nation in a State* (ed Brown, Ten Book Press, 2007) and *A Nation Again* (ed Henderson Scott, Luath Press, 2011).

Luath Press is an independently owned and managed book publishing company based in Scotland, and is not aligned to any political party or grouping. *Viewpoints* is an occasional series exploring issues of current and future relevance.

Arguing for Independence

Evidence, Risk and the Wicked Issues

STEPHEN MAXWELL

Luath Press Limited

EDINBURGH

www.luath.co.uk

First published 2012
Reprinted 2013

ISBN: 978-1908373-3-35

The author's right to be identified as author of this book under the Copyright, Designs and Patents Act 1988 has been asserted.

The paper used in this book is recyclable. It is made from low-chlorine pulps produced in a low energy, low emissions manner from renewable forests.

Printed and bound by
Martins the Printers, Berwick upon Tweed

Typeset in 11 point Sabon

Contents

Preface

Thomas Paine's *Common Sense* was the book which gave the American public their most urgent rationale for independence when it appeared in January 1776. Six months later, a majority of the delegates elected by the 13 rebellious British colonies to their Congress declared the independence of what they now called the United States of America. At the time Paine was writing, barely one third of the American people were likely to have favoured American independence.

Stephen Maxwell gave his life to the cause of Scottish independence, and devoted his last months to building that lifetime's research and thought into *Arguing for Independence*. He had finished it, given it for critiques and incorporated the most useful comments into his text when he died on 24 April 2012. The final work normally needed from an author has been done as best we could by his wife Sally, his younger son Jamie, and me, the friend with whom he worked on his last draft. We were greatly helped in our work by Harry McGrath, by Mark Thomson, and by Jim Eadie MSP, whose work in his SNP constituency (Edinburgh Southern) had been guided by Stephen. As always, our gratitude to the National Library of Scotland must be overwhelming.

Arguing for Independence lifts the entire debate on Scottish independence to a new intellectual level. Stephen was an austere scholar, and a teacher to the marrow of his bones. He left his politics tutorship at Edinburgh University to become SNP Press Officer in the mid-1970s, and his press briefings were probably unique: hostile journalists were staggered to hear him explain that their objections to this or that in the party were not really rewarding subjects but that a more useful question to raise would be this other. The Labour MP Norman Buchan, a chivalrous opponent, declared that while Stephen might satisfy his party in public relations, he would never settle for that himself but would always think deeper. Stephen intellectualised the first struggle for Scottish devolution up to the referendum of 1979 when a thin majority of voters supported a Scottish legislative assembly.

A lifelong Scottish Nationalist, Stephen warmly welcomed cooperation with other left-wingers in other parties, beginning with the 1979 referendum. He would have applauded the current independence campaign's muster of the Scottish Greens, the Scottish Socialists, and giants of the non-SNP Left such as Margo MacDonald and Dennis Canavan, as well as the SNP itself.

Stephen was a lifetime opponent of nuclear weapons, as indeed were so many SNP members. Among the very last words he said to me as we finished what would be our last conversation: 'Only independence can get Scotland clear of nuclear armaments. Anything less than independence will mean that a foothold for nuclear weapons will always remain.' Priorities of our people's lives instead of other people's deaths mean that what we save from what we now pay for weapons of mass destruction can help us to keep a truly just society alive.

The welfare state reformed a cruelly unequal pre-war British society but independence is now Scotland's only hope of preserving the National Health Service, the investment in our future given by free university education, and so much else where the UK led the world. Stephen's respect for our opponents' best work demands that we conserve Scotland's finest heritage. And it means drawing on real history, instead of some of the nonsense invented against independence. With independence it may be necessary for Scotland to stay in the sterling area; independent Ireland did it for 50 years. An independent Scotland puts the UK seat in the UN Security Council in no more danger than the end of the USSR and its loss of former possessions endangered Russia's seat; the UN is the continuation of the wartime alliance of the same name and the leading allies hold their places in perpetuity. Stephen insisted that the fight for independence would always be a fight against ignorance.

George Orwell's writings still warn us against the politicisation of vocabulary where war is described as peace, slavery as freedom, and ignorance as strength. Stephen stood for truth in all things, and while Orwell might have disagreed with some things in *Arguing for Independence*, he would have found the mind that made it as scrupulous as his own.

Devolution brought great benefits to Scottish culture, notably in helping to erode the Scottish cringe, the apparent Scottish conviction that one must never admit it, but others know best. This is changing so rapidly that in 2011 the Scottish voters did what almost all analysts were convinced could never happen, giving the SNP an overall majority in the Scottish Parliament. This was not a vote for independence. It was a vote for independent-mindedness: the voters wanted a Scottish government which made its own decisions rather than having the final say in party policy being subject to London commands and vetoes.

The long road to devolution escalated interest in Scottish history among academics and the wider public; nationalism has thus been the friend of Scottish historical research and writing, unlike in Ireland where nationalism's coarser prophets (from Charles Haughey to the IRA) were the enemies of reputable history. In part this stems from Ireland's drinking the poisoned chalice rejected from Scottish Nationalism by SNP decree: violence. Works such as Robert Crawford's *Devolving Scottish Literature* show the new and deeper focus in Scottish cultural studies. But in some respects devolution actually set back Scottish cultural progress, notably in areas reserved to UK administration, above all in broadcasting. Scottish theatre must also emancipate itself from its inability to give full confidence to fellow Scots. It had some of its greatest success in small touring companies (7:84 was the outstanding achievement, performing *The Cheviot, the Stag and the Black, Black Oil* before all Scotland). Today they show little sign of revival, as communities lose their identity before the all-devouring media in trivial innovation or meaningless repetition. As the Edinburgh Festival and Fringe have shown, Scotland wants the world, not some filtered down metropolitan trendiness. Stephen pointed to the Scots migration across the world and to the real cultures the world sent back to Scotland. Today the sheer economic fact of Scotland's need for immigrants divides her from England whose Home Office excludes and ejects from Scotland the people she needs and wants to welcome.

The ultimate cultural case for Scottish independence turns on the inflexible honesty intrinsic to Stephen. Scottish independence is tied to his principles: that a society taking its identity in the ownership of weapons of mass destruction forfeits the allegiance of civilised humans; that a society judging itself on cultural identity handed out by imperial preference or cosmopolitan fashion destroys itself; that a society which perpetually lives by imagining itself as the centre of empire actually long gone lives a lie it becomes toxic to inhabit; that a society which takes its pride in the ostentation of its wealth rather than the health of its poor is a society demanding repudiation; that a society whose artists cannot think of its own territory as the primary focus for love, for anger, for identity, for sheer self-expression, for disenchantment, above all for truth is a society twisted into contortions by obsessions with the outsider, market-maker, master. Stephen would never allow Scots to comfort themselves by blaming England. For him, independence always meant telling the truth to ourselves, about ourselves.

Arguing for Independence is Stephen's testament, and in the years lying ahead we will need to read and re-read it, for its arguments, for its ideals, for its humanity. Within its pages we will be perpetually rejuvenated by the spirit of the man who had willed it to us, one of the best, wisest and kindest people most of us have ever known. We will learn the strength of a small country knowing it is small, and thereby teaching without bullying, rather than blinding ourselves to the weakness of a small country thinking it is large, and therefore unable to learn, let alone teach. Let us welcome the light of what in every respect is Stephen Maxwell's *Common Sense*.

Owen Dudley Edwards, University of Edinburgh, July 2012

Acknowledgements

After more than 40 years' involvement in the debate on Scotland's political future, as a member and national press officer of the Scottish National Party, as an SNP parliamentary candidate and elected SNP councillor, as a Party Vice Chair and as a contributor over the decades to many periodicals and books on Scottish issues, I have accumulated debts to far more people than I can possibly acknowledge here.

Like everyone else in the Scottish debate I owe an intellectual debt to those writers who have put the independence movement in Scotland in its wider political and cultural contexts, in Britain and internationally, among them Tom Nairn, Neal Ascherson, Christopher Harvie, Neil MacCormick, Michael Keating, Lindsay Paterson and Paul Henderson Scott. I have been particularly fortunate from an Edinburgh base in having had the opportunity from time to time to exchange views face to face.

I owe a special debt to Owen Dudley Edwards not only for extending my understanding of the variety of nationalisms within the British Isles but also for his longstanding friendship which has included commenting on a late draft of this manuscript in an attempt to reduce the inaccuracies and solecisms it still contained. Needless to say any shortcomings which persist are entirely my own.

The many campaigners for independence alongside whom I have worked since the early seventies have had a greater influence than they can know, or perhaps would care to acknowledge, on the development of my own ideas on Scotland's independence. I am particularly grateful to Margo MacDonald, Jim Sillars and Isobel Lindsay. And I owe thanks to former colleagues and continuing friends in Scotland's voluntary sector for constantly reminding me of the real purpose and justification of constitutional change.

Finally I owe my wife Sally and children Luke, Katie and Jamie a greater debt than I can ever repay for their constant support and their encouragement to persevere with the book in difficult personal circumstances.

Introduction

The writing of this book spanned the SNP's stunning victory in the Scottish Parliament elections of May 2011. The outright majority achieved by the SNP transformed the context of the debate on Scottish independence. A referendum on independence which had previously been a SNP aspiration suddenly became a certainty.

The prospect induced a fever in Scotland's political class and media. An instant hue and cry was raised for the Scottish Government to set a date for the referendum, to decide the question and to define the details of the independence settlement, all within months of the SNP's victory. When the Scottish Government published a more considered timetable allowing for consultation on the timing, question and eligibility for voting, it was accused of manipulating the process to its own advantage.

The prelude to the referendum was always bound to be as political as the referendum campaign itself. The Unionists saw their interest in a quick referendum before the SNP's publicity machine could erode the Scottish voters' clear preference for the Union. And while the Scottish Government could claim a public interest in taking time to consult the electorate and inform the public of the mechanics and political implications of independence, it too had partisan interests at stake. In particular, it needed to clarify its own thinking on some of the more problematic issues for independence which the party, in its preoccupation with winning power in devolved Holyrood, had neglected. These included issues critical to public confidence such as the currency to be adopted and the fiscal credibility of an independent Scotland under the impact of the global financial crisis.

So the SNP's surprise election triumph set the stage for a phony 'pre-debate' from which we are only slowly emerging. The Unionists and their sceptical fellow travellers launched a stream of practically focused challenges. How could Scotland's credit rating absorb the weight of Scotland's debt legacy from the United Kingdom? How could Scotland be sure it would be admitted to the European Union? How could Scotland afford to start an Oil Fund when its budget would be in net fiscal deficit? How could it risk so much on unpredictable oil prices? Why should the Bank of England accept the role of lender of last resort within a shared currency area without imposing stringent budgetary controls incompatible with Scottish budgetary freedom? The clearest symptoms of the fever coursing through some Unionist veins was an anonymous suggestion from official sources that the rUK (rest of UK) Government might actually oppose Scotland's membership of the EU and even of the United Nations, and a call from Lord Fraser of Carmyllie, a former Tory Solicitor General for Scotland, that in the event of independence the UK's Trident nuclear submarine base should be offered to Orkney and Shetland, along with the northern oil fields, as an inducement to remain part of the Union (BBC Scotland *News*, 13/03/2012).

For someone in the middle of writing a book with the ambition of exploring the nature of the debate for independence and attempting to offer a reasoned case for independence under a range of headings, this stream of 'what ifs' and 'maybes', of wild surmises and crazy suppositions, posed a challenge. If the public debate was focusing on a mixture of practical short-term issues and deluded fantasies, would there be an audience for the longer term, strategic case for independence, focusing on the benefits beyond the first few years of independence? On the other hand, to allow the book to be dominated by an *à la carte* selection of real or imagined short term, sometimes transitional, dilemmas would divert it from my orginal purpose of presenting a case under different headings, weighing the evidence, as far as I was able, for and against.

My response has been pragmatic. An important part of my case is that any serious argument for independence needs to be multilayered, focused as much on the particulars of Scotland's circumstances as on general principles, and so what I judged to be the more serious of the media's favourite issues are absorbed into making each case for independence. The more tendentious issues of the sort that a canvasser for independence might face on the doorsteps and in the shopping malls are addressed in a Q&A under the heading 'Aye, but…'.

I am sure that determined opponents of independence will find my attempts to weigh the conflicting evidence to be corrupted by my support for independence. I fear too that many supporters of independence will miss the blithe confidence with which the case for independence was habitually proclaimed in the years when the prospect of its being tested at the ballot box seemed remote. I hope, nevertheless, that the arguments presented here will make their own distinctive contribution to the vigour of the debate on Scotland's political future which is now gathering momentum.

Stephen Maxwell, Edinburgh, March 2012

Ways of Arguing

Introduction

THIS SHORT BOOK ARGUES the case for Scottish independence. Over the last three decades there has been a broadening flow of writing inspired directly or indirectly by the emergence of Scottish Nationalism as a significant political force, contributed by political scientists, economists, cultural analysts, historians, constitutional theorists, writers of political memoirs and any number of 'state of the nation' pundits. But, perversely, the political and intellectual source of this flow – the proposition that Scotland should resume its political independence – has featured only modestly. Over the last 20 years, the number of books dedicated to elaborating a case for Scottish independence can be counted on the fingers of two hands. This book is a contribution to correcting that imbalance. It focuses primarily on the generic case for independence: that is, the benefits and disbenefits which would follow most directly from a move to independence. This necessarily involves some discussion of how the policies which might be pursued following independence could be expected to differ from those of the rest of the UK (rUK) but it stops well short of recommending a comprehensive policy platform for an independent Scotland. While there is undoubtedly a need for more debate about the policy options for an independent Scotland, a book with the primary aim of providing a rational, evidenced case for independence *per se* is not the place to offer it.

The case for independence is presented here under six headings – the democratic case, the economic case, the social case, the international case, the cultural case and the environmental case. An attempt is made to found each case on supportable claims about the disadvantages of Scotland's lack of independence on the one hand and the benefits which can reasonably be expected from independence on the other. That may sound a modest enough ambition but political argument is seldom straightforward.

Maxims and Facts

Political argument comes in many forms and the debate for and against Scotland's independence has utilised all of them. The framework of most political argument is provided by maxims, claims to general truths based on experience – 'that democracy is the worst form of government except for all the others', or 'the best form of government is self-government', or, topically, 'banks which are too big to fail are bad banks'.

Maxims always carry the qualification 'other things being equal'. But if a maxim is sufficiently well established it will carry an authority which puts the onus on the opponent to demonstrate why it does not apply to the case in question.

The authority of maxims derives from the belief that they correspond with the facts. Facts are the staple of political argument. Burns proclaimed in 'A Dream' (1786) that 'Facts are chiels that winna ding / And downa be disputed'.[1] He was too sanguine. In political argument facts are endlessly disputed. They have first to be distinguished from factoids – claims purporting to be facts which turn out to be nothing of the sort. Tony Blair's claims about Saddam Hussein's possession of weapons of mass destruction capable of being brought into action within 45 minutes are one example. But the discrediting of one fact is seldom decisive in political argument. When one fact falls, others are quickly conscripted to replace it. Thus, the case for invading Iraq shifted from the claim that Saddam possessed operational weapons of mass destruction to the claim that he had hidden armaments capable of being brought into action within weeks if not days, that if he did not have actual weapons he was actively pursuing weapons programmes, that if he did not have active programmes then he certainly had the ambition to have such programmes: by any token, he was failing fully to implement the terms of UN resolutions which would conclusively demonstrate that he did not have weapons or weapons programmes.

In the end, the case for the war was worn down by a combination of facts in which the absence of weapons of mass destruction and the number of US war-dead featured alongside estimates of Iraqi civilian deaths (but why only civilian deaths?) and the effect of the invasion in provoking the very terrorism it was designed to defeat.

The argument about Scottish independence has its own example of the inconclusive nature of appeals to facts. Until the discovery of large reserves of oil and gas in the Scottish province of the North Sea in the late 1960s and early '70s, arguments for Scotland's independence were widely dismissed on the grounds that Scotland was too poor to be independent. When the scale of the North Sea discoveries became apparent, supporters of independence believed that the argument that Scotland was too poor had been conclusively overturned. They were not alone. The Chief Economic Adviser to the Scottish Office agreed with them. In a secret memorandum to senior civil service colleagues in Whitehall, Dr Gavin McCrone wrote that 'the advent of North Sea oil has completely overturned the traditional economic argument used against Scottish nationalism' (McCrone, 1975).[2]

The discovery of the oil reserves turned out to be the beginning, not the end, of the argument about the economic benefits of independence. Opponents argued variously that the reserves would not last long, that Scotland did not have the capital resources or the engineering capacity to develop the reserves herself, and that even if she managed to establish control of the oil, the flow of revenues would ruin the competitiveness of the Scottish economy and destroy its export trade. Better that responsibility for the oil remain with the UK with its more experienced civil service and much greater economic capacity, not to mention its desperate need to support its balance of payments.

Forty years later, after the Scottish province has yielded around £270bn of revenues for the UK Treasury and with about half as much oil still to be extracted as has been pumped out in the last four decades, the argument that an independent Scotland would gain no net benefit from control of its oil reserves is still being made.

Ethical Claims

There is a strong ethical dimension to most political arguments. Precepts asserting ethical claims – 'nations ought to take responsibility for managing their own affairs', or 'it would be selfish to claim the financial benefits of Scotland's North Sea oil for ourselves' – are staples of the Scottish debate. In some contexts, precepts attract fundamentalist support, promoting them as moral absolutes regardless of the practical consequences of applying them. In the independence debate in

Scotland, it is more usual for precepts to carry an explicit or implicit reservation – 'Scots ought to take responsibility for their own future through independence – provided that independence is compatible with economic prosperity and/or maintaining Scotland's welfare state', or 'It would be selfish to claim North Sea oil for Scotland – at least if the UK uses the oil wealth responsibly'.

The ethical dimension often embraces claims about the moral worth of the policies an independent Scotland would pursue. 'An independent Scotland would not support neo-colonial adventures like the Iraq invasion', or 'An independent Scotland would insist on the removal of nuclear weapons bases from Scotland, not only freeing itself from an immoral and illegal policy but also forcing the rest of the UK into unilateral nuclear disarmament.' Or the counter: 'Independence would mean Scotland evading its responsibility for its own security and for freedom and democracy around the world while sheltering behind the nuclear skirts of the UK and the US.'

In domestic policy, Nationalists may claim that the left-of-centre bias of Scottish politics provides a more stable base for action against poverty and inequality than the bias of UK politics towards the centre-right. This is countered from the Unionist Left by accusations of abandoning the poor in the rest of the UK to the less progressive preferences of English voters. The ideological converse – that only independence will finally confront Scotland with the necessity to roll back its dependency on a bloated public sector – also features in the debate, though in a minor key.

Although there is no independent evidence of how far expectations of the ideological direction of an independent Scotland affect support for independence, the temper of public debate suggests that most Scots are content to have Scotland's ideological future determined by the democratic process within whatever constitutional structure the Scots choose for themselves. As with most moral arguments within a broad community of values, appeals to the facts in the form of the predicted consequences are as important as appeals to the moral principles themselves.

International Comparisons

The experience of other countries is often cited in the independence debate. 'An independent Scotland could emulate the success of the Nordic countries', or, since the advent of the global financial crisis, 'An independent Scotland would have suffered the fate of Ireland and Iceland'. International comparisons provide suggestive models of small country successes or failures. They provide historical perspective and they offer examples of specific policy options. But because the history and hence the overall situation of each country is unique, the relevance of such comparisons will always be contestable, and so need specific justification.

Facts and Theory

As we have seen, facts often make their presence felt in popular political debate in the shape of maxims. But they also come embedded in political theory. One of the fashionable themes of political analysis in recent decades has been the growth of international interdependence, often glossed as globalisation. It is easy for unwary readers to be persuaded that the principles of politics which analysts discover in the facts are more like rules than hazardous generalisations, and that when experts conclude that global interdependence makes political independence irrelevant or impossible for small countries, they have uncovered a universal or even a prescriptive truth behind the facts. Of course, even the most ambitious explanatory theory, in political science no less than natural science, depends on facts – distilled, correlated, juxtaposed, manipulated – but always correctable by other facts. The extent to which political independence in an interdependent world is functional or dysfunctional for a political community remains to be determined by the facts of the particular case, not by general principles.

Uncertainty and Probability

The sorts of argumentation – maxim, precept, facts in all their guises – deployed in the independence debate cannot be expected, singly or in combination, to establish a conclusion beyond doubt. Claims for a political proposition need to be judged in terms of probability. The question is whether the degree of uncertainty which is unavoidably attached to a political proposition is at a level which undermines its claim to be a sufficient reason for action.

As an exercise in induction, political reasoning is especially problematic. The analogy is not with legal argument which seeks to establish the facts 'beyond reasonable doubt'. Because the bulk of the argumentation on both sides of the independence debate is about a hypothetical situation – what the effects would be if Scotland were to become an independent state – no direct evidence is available. In legal argument, circumstantial evidence can satisfy the test of 'beyond reasonable doubt'. But the vast complexity of political argument means that there will always be scope for reasonable doubt. A closer analogy is with the everyday judgements we make between the value of a desired outcome and the risks we are willing to take to secure it. We fancy a holiday in Mexico. But to get there means incurring some level of risk: suppose the plane comes down mid-Atlantic or we succumb to some exotic infection? Reflecting on the risks may make us think again about whether being in Mexico would be sufficiently rewarding after all. If the attractions of Mexico retain their appeal we make a judgement about the probability of our plane going down as of other less catastrophic eventualities, before reaching a judgement of the balance between the anticipated benefit and the risks.

The financial crisis and ensuing economic recession have placed the question of risk at the centre of the independence debate. Defenders of the Union argue that the more autonomy Scotland enjoys, the greater the risks to which Scotland will be exposed as, for example, the risk under fiscal autonomy of being unable to fund vital public services and under independence, the risk of financial collapse on an Icelandic or Irish scale. It is true that for nations, as for individuals, independence means the cost of failure might sometimes be higher. But just as most individuals choose independence over dependence because they believe that its promise of more benefit and satisfaction outweighs the risks, so nations may face a choice between a safe but constraining dependence and a riskier but more fulfilling independence. As always, the rational option is to be found not in the principles but in a judgement of the balance of risks and anticipated benefits in the particular case.

One of the persistent dividing lines between constitutional conservatives and constitutional radicals in the independence debate is their differing treatment of risk over time. Typically, conservatives discount the claim of significant medium or long-term benefits from independence or greater economic autonomy against the short-term risks, while radicals tend to discount the short-term risks against the anticipated longer-term benefits. So claims by the radicals that Scots could use the wider state powers available to them under self-government progressively to accumulate public benefit for the nation are met by warnings that such gains can never be guaranteed and that meantime an increase in the budget deficit threatens for next year.

Conservatives and radicals can agree that in politics nothing can be guaranteed, whether for the constitutional status quo or for constitutional change. But that does not reduce political disagreement to an irresolvable difference of political temperament as between long-term optimists and short-term pessimists. The disagreement can, in principle, be resolved rationally by assessing the specifics of the case against the relevant evidence to establish the probability of the claimed outcomes. For example, the short-term risk of fiscal autonomy leading to a major budget deficit because of annual variations in oil revenues can be weighed against a judgement of the probability of Scotland being able to borrow against the security of her energy assets in an era of rising energy prices. Conversely, the probability of long-term benefits created by the policy changes which independence would make possible can be assessed against the short-term risks of change in the midst of global financial crisis.

So the case argued here does not claim to provide a certainty of increased benefit from independence. It accepts that there will always be some doubt but argues that the evidence in all its diversity and complexity establishes a sufficiently strong probability of major benefit, for future if not present generations of Scots, to meet the balance of benefit over risk which most of us apply in our everyday lives, as when we decide to book that holiday in Mexico.

The Confidence Issue

For some people, the fact that the argument for independence cannot deliver certainty will be an insuperable obstacle. Just as there are some who deny themselves the pleasures of long distance travel because they are unwilling to take the risk of flying, there are some Scots whose aversion to risk is so strong that they will be deaf to a case for independence based on probability, however strong. There is a view asserted sometimes by frustrated Nationalists and sometimes by pessimistic Unionists that Scots are victims of a general 'crisis of confidence' which, by making them especially averse to risk, limits their individual and collective capacities to improve their lives. As a general theory the proposition suffers from the difficulty of defining such a complex phenomenon as confidence and is questioned by the existence of very many personally confident Scots, though it remains a possibility that the Scottish population contains a larger minority of individuals suffering from a chronic lack of personal confidence than the populations of other comparably developed societies (Craig, 2003).[3]

The claim that Scotland's public culture, perhaps more specifically its political culture, suffers from a deficit of confidence is more plausible. But here the causes are more likely to be found in Scotland's institutional history and the remedies in reforming those institutions. In any event the case for independence presented here assumes the existence of a Scottish public equipped to make a rational choice for or against independence. If people decline to engage with the debate, or having engaged, decline to be persuaded for independence, then it is more reasonable to conclude that the case advanced is insufficiently persuasive or that the issue is not of sufficient interest to them than that they are somehow incapable by virtue of their individual or national psychology of giving it rational consideration.

Political arguments are brought to a resolution not on paper or across the debating floor but by actions, at best the decision of voters, at worst the use of force, and such resolutions usually have only a tangential relationship with the merits of the reasoned case. There is no impartial arbiter to announce one protagonist the winner by virtue of better sourced evidence or superior logic. Because the supply of possibly relevant facts is inexhaustible, the argument from evidence may continue long after the issue has been settled in practical terms. The question of how the Treaty of Union of 1707 was secured, and whether its consequences for Scotland were on balance positive or negative continues to be debated to this day. If this discourse were to generate a clear consensus it might affect how some Scots today felt about independence. But this 'affect' could never substitute for the empirically-based debate for or against independence.

Belonging and Identity

To some, the attempt to present a rational, empirically justified case for Scottish independence is doomed to fail because Nationalism is about 'blood and belonging', about instinct and emotion, not reason. There have certainly been Nationalisms where the appeal to racial or other identities have drowned out whatever rational case may have been made for or against change. Within the last two decades the Balkans and Rwanda offer themselves as obvious examples of conflicts fuelled by 'blood and belonging' though even in such extreme cases a factual claim has often been the trigger for, if not the ultimate cause of the conflict. And often the containment or resolution of the conflict has included a process of challenging the factual base of accepted narratives (Ignatieff, 1995).[4]

'I have always been deeply ambivalent about Nationalism,' answered the playwright Alistair Beaton to a question about whether he thought the SNP would like his new play *Caledonia* about the Darien Scheme premiered at the 2010 Edinburgh International Festival (*The Herald*, 19/03/2010).[5] He misunderstood the nature of Nationalism. Nationalism is not a single phenomenon. In political and cultural content there as many Nationalisms as there are national communities attempting to exercise self-determination. It is perfectly reasonable to be suspicious of some categories of Nationalism on the evidence of their record – say big-state Nationalism, ethnic Nationalism or right-wing Nationalism – while being favourably disposed towards other categories – small-state Nationalism, civic Nationalism or welfare Nationalism. But to establish whether any particular Nationalist claim for self-determination is deserving of support it's essential to examine its particular content and circumstances. The question in the Scottish debate is not about the nature of Nationalism but about a particular claim for independence.

Positive Rights

The case for independence is sometimes presented as a claim of a right to self-determination. However, despite the inclusion in Article 1 of the United Nations Charter (1945) of a reference to the 'equal rights and self-determination of peoples', and an apparently more definitive assertion in Article 1 of the International Covenant on Civil and Political Civil Rights (1966) that 'All peoples have the right of self-determination', there is no general acceptance among international or human rights lawyers that people living within the territory of an existing and recognised sovereign state have an absolute right to secede. The UN's references to self-determination are usually interpreted rather as reminders of the obligation of existing states to respect the rights of other states or as an assertion of the rights of peoples living under colonial rule (Robertson, 2002).[6]

The decision of the International Court of Justice in the summer of 2010 that Kosovo's secession from Serbia was not illegal may have shifted the balance towards an inherent right of national self-determination but it still leaves plenty of scope for dispute (International Court of Justice website, 2011).[7] It continues to be best to treat the right to political independence of a people living within a state as full and equal citizens (as the Scots do more or less in the UK), as a presumptive right, drawing on democratic principle rather than international human rights law, but still needing to be justified in its specific context.

In practice, whatever the technical legal arguments, successive UK political leaders have conceded the right of Scotland to withdraw from the Union if a majority of Scots vote to do so. That leaves to be answered the question addressed in these pages – with or without a legal right would it be right morally and pragmatically for Scots to opt for independence?

Identity and Community

Most campaigners for Scotland's independence are not driven primarily by linguistic or ethnic concerns but by a desire for a more responsive and effective form of Scottish Government. That does not mean that they may not bring strong emotions to their advocacy. Many Scots, Nationalist or not, will have a sense of historic grievance against England, or feel frustration at Scotland's slow social and economic progress within the UK, or anger at what they see as the indifference or ignorance of London Governments to Scotland's best opportunities for development. Some may feel that the balance of political and cultural power under which they lives denies them recognition as Scots or simply as people living in a community with its particular geography, history and cultures. Others may draw their ambition for change from a sense of how much better a place to live in Scotland could be as an independent country: hope for the future can be as strong an emotion as grievance at past injustices or indifferent government. But neither anger at the past nor hope for the future makes a case. That stands or falls on the strength of the evidence of the benefits and disbenefits of independence in the particular case.

Scottish Nationalism is often presented as a search for Scottish identity or nationality. Scotland is indisputably a nation and the majority of the people who live in Scotland identify themselves as Scottish (Bechhofer and McCrone, 2009).[8] But why they identify as Scots *not* British, or Scots *and* British, or any of the other permutations is hard to determine. William McIlvanney has written: 'Having a national identity is a bit like having an old insurance policy. You know you've got one somewhere but often you're not entirely sure where it is. And if you're honest, you would have to admit you're pretty vague about what the small print means' (McIlvanney, 1999).[9] If a majority in a society has a clear sense of national identity, then that identity may provide a sufficient base from which to mobilise significant support for independence, as in Québec. But it cannot play more than a secondary role in a reasoned case for independence. In Scotland it is clear that the majority of those who identify themselves as Scots would be hard pressed to provide a definition of Scottish identity which would be acceptable to the next half dozen self-identifying Scots they met on the street. Attempts to define Scottish identity or nationality between native Scots are far more likely to start an argument than to gain assent. In this, the Scots are similar to their English, Welsh and Irish neighbours in the British Isles.

Benedict Anderson presents Nationalism as rooted in a shared 'imagined community' (Anderson, 1983).[10] What 'imagined community' do Scots share? Evidently not a community focused on a distinctive dominant language which defines or symbolises a national culture. Nor can an 'imagined community' easily be reconstructed from the myths and remembered fragments of Scotland's history. Seventy years ago Edwin Muir found such material wanting – 'Wallace and Bruce guard now a painted field, / And all may read the folio of our fable'. (Muir, 1960).[11] And the subcultures of anglo-atlanticised, multi-ethnic, globalised

Scotland are unlikely to be charmed into community by the lurid appeal of a Hollywood *Braveheart*. As Anderson argued, the search for community will usually belong more to a functional future than to a bowdlerised past.

In the traditional account, the Scots' sense of community was attached to the national institutions entrenched by the Union settlement – the Church, Scots law and education – reinforced by such later growths as the Scottish regiments, Scottish football and the Scottish press. But in their varying stages of decline these are waning sources of community. The creation of a Scottish Parliament has introduced a new and pushy rival to traditional Scottish civil society as an influence on Scots' sense of identity, but in an era of alienation from conventional politics the Parliament's potential to serve as a focus for a revived sense of Scottish community remains unproven.

Perhaps the best place to look for an 'imagined community' north of the border is where fragments of inherited Scottish identity overlap with emerging senses of community: a political community nurtured by devolution and by the divergence of voting patterns north and south of the border; a moral or civil community increasingly at odds with the grand illusions and archaisms of Great Britain; a community of self-assertiveness which insists that in the era of cultural anarchy promoted by the communications' revolution, Scottish voices must either make themselves heard in the global babel, or be crowded out of the minds, and eventually even the memory, of those who live in Scotland.

National identity is usually learned as a personal or family story. It may carry with it a sense of wider belonging and community but it seldom determines political attitudes. In the Scottish debate the role of national identity is best limited to two secondary roles – as one strand of a cultural argument for independence and in support of a claim that independence would strengthen Scots self-confidence.

If Scottish Nationalism is less about identity and more about agency – how to improve life in Scotland for all those who live here, regardless of their cultural or national identities – then that reinforces the need for a rational, evidenced case for independence. It is easier to elaborate this as a way of improving people's lives in Scotland than as a way of reinforcing or giving expression to their sense of Scottishness.

One of the ironies is that in recent years the opponents of Scottish independence have been more likely to appeal to a confected sense of

British nationality and identity in the cause of the Union than have Scottish Nationalists in the cause of independence. As Chancellor and then as Prime Minister, Gordon Brown put the promotion of British identity and values at the centre of his political strategy, in the face of widespread indifference and no little ridicule north and south (Brown, 2006; Ascherson, 2008).[12]

None of this should be read as a denial of Scottish identity or nationality. Those who are of Scottish upbringing will recognise signals of language and mood, rhythms of thought and feeling, 'accents of the mind', that people of English or Welsh other upbringing may miss. And there is clear evidence that those Scots who declare a primary Scottish identity – Scottish not British – are more likely than other Scots to join the SNP though among SNP voters the proportion falls to only 45% (Mitchell, 2012).[13] But reflecting the jumbled ethnic and cultural composition of Scotland's population today and the diversity of external influences it is exposed to, Scottish identity is too eclectic and complex to provide the grounding for a case for independence.

The lack of a 'given' national identity and of a distinctive language in common use is sometimes cited as a weakness of Scottish Nationalism, compared to contemporary Nationalisms in Québec or Catalonia and even Wales. But it is the total context that is important. Where a distinctive identity or language is shared by a majority or at least a significant section of the population, then it can provide an electoral base and support a case for independence.

Most developed societies today, not excluding the three examples above, are to a significant extent multicultural so limiting the force of an appeal to linguistic or national identity or even turning it into a source of division. Wherever a common identity is invoked as a foundation for a claim for constitutional empowerment it will, in practice, be balanced against people's judgement of what economic or other gains or losses pursuing the claim will bring. A case for a change of political status requires political justification. In any event, most Scots seem content to accept McIlvanney's description of Scotland as 'our mongrel nation'. (McIlvanney, 1992).[14] In such a nation, advocates of independence can pitch their democratic and pragmatic arguments for independence at all of their fellow citizens whatever identities they may profess in public or nurture within their own communities.

I hope that the pragmatic, evidenced case for Scottish independence made here will have some appeal to those who feel more British than Scottish, and to those who resist pigeonholing their identity at all, as well as to those who feel Scottish rather than British or equally Scottish and British. As an argument based mainly on the benefits of democratic self-determination as the surest way to good government and a vigorous public culture, there is no reason, though there may be sufficient cause, why it should not appeal also to those who feel British *not* Scottish.

References

1 Burns, R, 'A Dream' in Kinsley, J (ed), *The Poems and Songs of Robert Burns*, Vol. 1. Oxford, 1968.

2 McCrone, G, *The Economics of Nationalism Re-Examined*. Scottish Economic Planning Department, Scottish Office, 1975.

3 Craig, C, *The Scots' Crisis of Confidence*. Glasgow, 2003.

4 Ignatieff, M, *Blood and Belonging: Journeys into the New Nationalism*. New York, 1995.

5 Beaton, A, *The Herald,* 19/03/2010.

6 Robertson, G, *Crimes Against Humanity: the Struggle for Global Justice,* London, 2002.

7 International Court of Justice website, 2011.

8 Bechhofer, F and McCrone, D, *Stating the Obvious: Ten Truths about National Identity*. Scottish Affairs No. 67, spring 2009.

9 McIlvanney, W, *The Herald,* 06/03/1999.

10 Anderson, B, *Imagined Communities: Reflections on the Origin and Spread of Nationalism*. London, 1983.

11 Muir, E, *Collected Poems*. London, 1960.

12 Brown, G, *The Future of Britishness*. The Fabian Society, 2006; Ascherson, N, 'The Future of an Unloved Union' in Devine, T (ed) *Scotland and the Union 1707–2007*. Edinburgh University Press, 2008.

13 Mitchell, J, Bennie, L and Johns, R, *The SNP in Transition to Power*. Oxford University Press, 2012.

14 McIlvanney, W, *Speech to the Campaign for a Scottish Assembly*. Edinburgh, 1992.

The Democratic Case

Introduction

SCOTS ALREADY ENJOY the classic rights and freedoms of democracy – freedom of opinion and belief, equality under the law, the right to vote, the right to property. Many of these rights were first won under the Union with England. So how can there be a democratic case for independence? There are several reasons. While the classic freedoms are the foundations of democracy whatever the scale and structure of the political unit in which they exist, the freedoms have two other important roles – to underpin effective government by the people for the people and to support a vigorous public culture.

Representative Government

The right to vote is important because it empowers people to choose governments which reflect their own priorities and values. But for 27 of the first 64 years after the Second World War, Scotland was ruled from Westminster by governments it had rejected at the polls. Eleven of those years were under the leadership of Mrs Thatcher who at her first general election in 1979 won only 22 Scottish seats out of 71 with 31% of the Scottish popular vote and at her third and final election in 1987, won only 10 seats out of 72 with 24% of the vote. The six years of Conservative rule which followed the ousting of Mrs Thatcher as Prime Minister in 1990 saw Conservative fortunes in Scotland stabilise temporarily before a further decline in the 1997 election when they won no seats at all in Scotland, attracting just 17% of the Scottish vote.

In the 2010 election the Conservatives won just one Scottish seat and 17% of the Scottish vote. The Conservative-Liberal Democrat Government at Westminster is a coalition of two minority Scottish parties which between them gained only 36% of the Scottish vote against a combined SNP and Labour vote of 63%. But if the Coalition survives for five years, Scotland will have been governed from Westminster by parties it rejected for 32 of the 70 post-war years. Furthermore, each of the Westminster Governments rejected by Scottish voters since 1970 – the Governments led by Heath, Thatcher, Major, and Cameron – has been distinctly to the right of Scottish political opinion. Indeed it could be argued that from the Heath Government on each of these rejected Governments has been progressively more hostile to the democratically expressed Scottish interest.

The years of Mrs Thatcher's government of Scotland exacted a particularly high price from Scotland's economy and society. Scottish rates of unemployment and poverty doubled and Scottish manufacturing employment fell by one third. Adding insult to the injuries, Mrs Thatcher's Governments enjoyed a massive £160bn inflow of revenues from North Sea oil (at 2008 prices) overwhelmingly from the Scottish sector of the North Sea oil province. (Commission on Scottish Devolution, 2009).[1] Many economists, from William Keegan in 1985 on, have suggested that it was North Sea oil that allowed Mrs Thatcher to meet the public bill for her disastrous monetarist experiment of 1979–81 which proved so destructive (Keegan, 1985).[2]

The cuts in public expenditure on which the Conservative–Liberal Democrat Coalition Government is now embarked far exceed Mrs Thatcher's declared ambitions. Whether the social consequences will be as damaging remains to be seen, though it is clear that it will be the poorest in Scottish society who will, again, be most vulnerable. The Independent Budget Report estimated that to 2025 over £40bn will be stripped from Scottish spending budgets (Scottish Government, 2010).[3] In the same period, under the current constitutional arrangements, Scotland's oil is likely to generate at least £70bn of revenues for the London Treasury.

Second-rate Democracy

The second democratic reason for preferring independence is that while the UK meets most of the formal criteria for democracy it does so only at a basic level. When Scotland went into the Union, England was a pioneer in the development of parliamentary government and the rule of law. By the end of the 18th century, she had lost that leadership and has never regained it. Today the UK is one of the least democratic of the world's established democracies. It lacks a written constitution defining the powers of the different levels of government, beginning with the Westminster Parliament which continues to enjoy many of the sovereign prerogatives which were once restricted to England's monarchs. It has continued to award a role in law making to an unelected second chamber composed of Government appointees who are usually party veterans, a selection of hereditary peers elected by their peers, and, most extraordinary of all, 26 bishops of the Church of England. At best, the Coalition's proposals for reform will replace this mix with a system of list elections which will preserve much of the power of patronage of the party hierarchies.

The first-past-the-post electoral system for the House of Commons regularly returns large overall majorities in the Commons for parties that have won only a minority of the popular vote. Indeed, since the Second World War, no single party government at Westminster has enjoyed a majority of the popular vote even when it has won a large majority of parliamentary seats, as the Conservatives did between 1979 and 1992 and the Labour Party did between 1997 and 2010. As the price of their participation in the coalition, the Liberal Democrats were given a referendum on the Alternative Vote, a system previously described by Liberal Democrat leader Nick Clegg as 'a miserable little compromise', which they lost ignominiously.

To add to the shortcomings of democracy Westminster-style, state power remains more highly centralised in the UK than in many younger democracies. The US, Canada, Australia, Spain, Germany, Italy, France, Belgium and the Netherlands have decentralised power, most often within federal constitutions, to state provinces or regional, municipal or communal authorities or most often some combination of these. By contrast, the most ambitious decentralisation in the UK has been the devolution at the end of the 1990s of strictly limited powers to Scotland, Wales and Northern Ireland, all subject to recall by Westminster under the doctrine of parliamentary sovereignty. The recently declared interest among UK politicians in transferring new powers to local authorities and even directly to voters in the shape of a popular power of recall of unsatisfactory MPs falls far short of a credible agenda for the decentralisation of power.

As a result of the pressures for constitutional change from the UK's national regions beginning with the Northern Ireland border referendum in 1973, the UK has been forced to accept that popular referenda have a role to play in its democracy. But its unease with the challenge which referenda pose to the traditional supremacy of the Westminster Parliament is shown in its reluctance to expose the greatest single constitutional issue it has faced since the Second World War to the test of public opinion. Twenty of the EU's 27 members have had referenda at some stage of their engagement with the Union; Ireland has had no fewer than six and Denmark has had four. The UK is the only one of the 20 whose sole referendum was after the constitutional fact: it was held in 1975, two years after the UK formally joined the Common Market. It was the product not of a constitutional provision designed to enshrine the right of the people to have their say on their constitutional future but because one of the Westminster party diarchy needed to avert a damaging and perhaps fatal split. It was, of course, non-mandatory. Over three decades later, despite repeated manifesto promises and half promises and a succession of changes in the membership, structure and legal powers of the European Union, Westminster politicians continue to avoid giving the voters their say (NSD European Election Database, 2011).[4]

The tepid enthusiasm for democratic reform among the majority of UK politicians can these days be taken as a given. More shocking to progressive opinion in the UK has been the eagerness of recent UK Governments to erode some of the classic liberties and rights in law of the British citizen. In truth the movement has not been all in one direction. The incorporation of the European Convention on Human Rights into UK law (2000), the creation of various ombudsmen offering redress to the citizen against administrative injustices (from 1967), a measure of freedom of information (2000) and the extension of equalities legislation from the Equal Pay Act 1967 to the Equality Act 2007 and beyond, reflect a continuing interest in the extension of citizens' rights. But the support of Labour Governments for ASBOS, the extension of detention without charge, limitations on trial by jury, the introduction of ID cards and a national data base, the holding of DNA samples by the police on people acquitted or never charged, and their stubborn opposition to the release to the courts of CIA documents revealing the collusion of UK security officials in the use of torture to extract information from detainees have dismayed many on the liberal Left who believed that while Labour might abandon socialism it would surely never compromise the core civil freedoms. While some of these policies, including ID cards and the National Data Base, have been dropped by the Coalition Government others such as 28-day detention without charge and control orders remain in place. A written constitution seems as distant as ever.

Meanwhile, the shortcomings of Westminster democracy in scrutinising the executive have disappointed not just liberals but democrats of all colours. The failure of both the Cabinet and Parliament properly to interrogate a Prime Minister evidently intent on an Iraq war of doubtful legality, to prevent him from prosecuting the war or to censure him afterwards, reveals a system incapable of performing its most basic duty of holding the executive accountable to the voters. Against failure on this historic scale, the revelations in 2009 that many MPs had for decades colluded in defrauding their expenses system seemed almost banal.

These weaknesses in the political institutions of UK democracy are compounded by the extreme centralisation of media and cultural power in the UK. One of the consequences for Scottish democracy was vividly illustrated in the 2010 general election when a cabal of UK political parties and broadcasters determined that the first ever general election debates between the leaders of UK political parties to be broadcast would be restricted to the leaders of the three main London-based political parties, excluding the leaders of the Nationalist parties in Wales and Scotland, as well as of other UK-wide contestants. This decision awarded the three biggest UK-wide political parties a combined four and a half hours of access to Scottish and Welsh voters free of direct challenge from representatives of the Nationalist parties in Wales and Scotland. The fact that voters in Wales and Scotland were provided with additional debates between the leaders of their territorial parties, including the UK-wide parties, did nothing to redress the balance, particularly as the UK leaders' debates, as predicted, dominated the general election campaign as a whole.

The London political leaders and broadcasters justified this stitch-up on the grounds that as the leaders of the Nationalist parties were not bidding to become the UK's Prime Minister, they had no claim to be included. They had either forgotten or simply chose to ignore that under the British constitution the role of general elections is to elect the legislature, not the executive: once elected, the Commons, with a bit of ritual help from the monarch, choose the executive. Ironically, the London cabal's decision to accelerate the UK's progress towards a presidential system of government came after two decades of decline in the share of the vote won by the two main UK parties and at a time when the polls indicated a distinct possibility of a hung Parliament in which the minor parties excluded from the UK leaders' debate might have had a deciding vote in the choice of a Government.

Given this record, it is not surprising that the UK's democratic credentials have lost their shine. The *Economist* Intelligence Unit's 2010 Democracy Index ranks the UK at 19th-equal with Spain as a Full Democracy skirting relegation to the category of a Flawed Democracy along with France, Italy and South Africa. The Nordic countries lead the rankings with five of the top 10 Full Democracy places (*Economist* Intelligence, Unit, 2010).[5]

Defective Pragmatism

The Unionist response to the growing democratic deficit in Scottish government within the UK caused by the divergence of voting patterns north and south of the border was devolution: devolving powers to a Scottish Parliament over a range of what were deemed domestic policy areas with a grant from the Westminster Parliament to pay for them would set the Scots free to pursue their own policy preferences, whatever electoral choices English voters made.

The response carried the hallmark of British pragmatism but in retrospect looks hopelessly naive. Unionist opponents quickly revived the 1979 West Lothian question – why should Scottish MPs be entitled to vote on domestic English affairs when English MPs could no longer vote on domestic Scottish issues? That question remains unanswered. Most supporters of independence, on the other hand, were prepared to accept devolution in the expectation that its limitations would quickly be exposed. Despite these unresolved tensions, in the first eight years of devolution (1999–2007), while Scotland benefited from its Barnett share of the Blair and Brown boom in public spending, devolution seemed to have realised the hopes of its Unionist founders. The Scottish Parliament legislated for a range of distinctive policies, including free social care, mental health and adult incapacity, the elimination of homelessness, electoral reform for local government and a charity law providing, for the first time in the UK, a test of public benefit.

But the Nationalists did not have long to wait. By the time of the 2007 Parliament elections, public frustration at the slow pace of change under Labour and Labour–Liberal Democrat administrations allied to growing fears about future economic prospects swung enough support behind the SNP to make it the largest single party. Following its move into Government the SNP launched its campaign for independence. Its paper *Choosing Scotland's Future* began by welcoming Scotland's achievement in recovering a 'direct democratic voice' through the Scotland Act of 1998 and presented the devolved Parliament as a jumping-off point for independence, referencing the Act's provision that any powers which were not specifically reserved to Westminster should be assumed to belong to the Scottish Parliament as an acknowledgement of Scotland's sovereign right (Scottish Government, 2007).[6]

The Unionist response had a very different tone. The Commission on Scottish Devolution (the Calman Commission), established jointly by the three Unionist parties in Scotland and the UK Government, made no direct reference to Scotland's democratic claims. Its remit was to recommend any changes to the UK's constitutional arrangements that would enable the Scottish Parliament to 'serve the people of Scotland better, improve the financial accountability of the Scottish Parliament, and continue to secure the position of Scotland within the UK'. The reference to financial accountability was the closest the remit came to acknowledging Scotland's democratic claims but its ambiguity was telling. Improve the financial accountability of the Parliament to whom – the Scottish people or the Westminster Government? The survey evidence did not suggest that a lack of accountability was a problem between the Scottish voters and the Scottish Parliament (Scottish Social Attitudes Survey, 2010).[7] As is evident in their final report the Commissioners seem to have been more interested in increasing the incentives for the Scottish Parliament and voters to manage Scotland's finances more responsibly than to increase their democratic control (Commission on Scottish Devolution, 2009).[8]

Against the market bias of the New Labour Government in its last two years of power, the new Scottish Government consolidated its appeal to Scotland's social democratic centre by defending an integrated NHS in Scotland, opposing the introduction of university fees and committing to end prescription charges. The strategy paid off handsomely for the SNP when the outcomes of the UK general election of 2010 and the 2011 Scottish Parliament elections revived the contrast between a neo-liberal English conservative majority which won Lib-Dem support, and a social democratic Scottish majority. With Scotland's Barnett grant from Westminster facing a cut of 12% in current spending and a cut of 36% to 2015 in capital spending, the promise that devolution would secure the democratic self-government of Scotland suddenly looked hollow (Scottish Government 2010).[9] Despite Scotland's political difference, despite her healthier fiscal balances as reported by the *Government Expenditure and Revenue in Scotland (GERS)* reports 2004–10, despite a buoyant trend in oil prices and the emerging potential of her green energy, the most a devolved Scotland could hope for was to mitigate at the margins the impact of Westminster's draconian response to the UK's budget crisis (Scottish Government, 2004; 2012).[10]

Democracy Beyond Devolution

When the proposals for devolution were being developed some Unionists believed that, in the words of the then Scottish Shadow Secretary George Robertson, devolution 'will kill Nationalism stone dead'. Robertson's view drew support from opinion surveys which showed that a clear majority of Scots preferred devolution to independence. He failed to take into account that many Scots were open-minded about how devolution might evolve, an attitude better understood by some of his party colleagues, possibly including Donald Dewar who was to become the first First Minister of Scotland (Davies, 1999).[11]

In the minds of some Unionists and academic analysts, devolution is part of a double lock on Nationalists' ambitions for independence. In their view, Scottish voters' consistent preference for devolution reflects the reality of the modern world, namely that globalisation – the growth of multilevel interdependence between societies around the world – limits the freedom of all states while bearing down with particular weight on small states. One consequence is that small states cannot in reality exert democratic control beyond their domestic affairs and even in domestic affairs their control is fragile. Denied the substance of independence, better that Nationalists abandon their illusions and reconcile themselves to working to maximise Scotland's powers within the UK or some wider European regional framework (Keating, 2009; 2011).[12]

The argument contains important truths but goes too far in generalising their implications. The important truths are that global interdependence limits the power of all states unilaterally to secure their preferred outcomes, domestic as well as external, and that the system is asymmetrical. Global interdependence is managed through a complex system of tradeoffs between states, only patchily disciplined by law or international institutions, in which larger states typically have more power in setting the terms than smaller states. But the conclusion that political independence has become irrelevant or somehow impossible for small states does not follow.

Part of the confusion arises from identifying independence with autarchy or self-sufficiency. In today's world even the largest states are not self-sufficient. China, or the US, or perhaps Russia might make themselves economically self-sufficient for a period, but only at the cost of long-term decline as a result of cutting off from the dynamism of other economies and cultures. For the great majority of states in the second or third rank of world power, including Germany, France and the UK, self-sufficiency is barely conceivable. Their positions on the spectrum of autarchy-interdependence overlap with those of the smaller advanced countries such as the Nordic countries, Switzerland, Austria, Canada and Australia, in an arc where their prospects for effective independence depend on their particular combination of geo-strategic location, natural, political and social assets.

A second source of confusion is the concept of sovereignty. As ascribed to states, sovereignty is the possession of an effective monopoly over the use of violence within the territory of the state. In this definition, it is conventionally accepted as a necessary condition for the recognition of a country's claim to full membership of the international community.

The monopoly on the use of violence is the condition for what has historically been the core claim of sovereignty – an exclusive right to make laws within the territory of the state. The right was at its strongest between the 17th and 19th centuries but has been in retreat since the 20th century as global interdependence, with its accompanying networks of institutions designed to manage interdependence, has advanced. Today national sovereignty is conventionally construed as consistent with participation in structures of global governance based on shared decision taking. Indeed, most claims for recognition as an independent state presume an ambition by the claimant to assume membership of certain key institutions of global governance along with whatever limitations on national sovereignty that entails. So whatever independence appears to require when viewed as an expression of an abstract principle of sovereignty, in today's world it is widely accepted as consistent with limitations on the exercise of sovereignty.

But even in an era of globalisation, participation in the institutions of global governance is presumed but not enforced. States are free to join or not to join the World Trade Organisation (WTO), the International Telecommunications Union (ITU), the Bank for International Settlements (BIS), the International Atomic Energy Agency (IAEA), the United Nations (UN) and the many other institutions which make up the web of global management. Even the International Criminal Court (ICC), charged with securing compliance with the most fundamental humanitarian laws, remains a voluntary membership body whose authority to take action against citizens of states not in membership is disputed.

To champions of globalisation such permissiveness may appear as an unfortunate lapse from the norms of global good government, but it signals a surviving acceptance that national sovereignty remains the foundation of the international community even in age of interdependence. In part this survival reflects the self-interest of states, not least the larger states, in retaining their international freedom of manoeuvre. But it also draws support from the historically more recent growth of national sovereignty's democratic alter ego, the idea of popular sovereignty as the ultimate source of the freedom of nations in international as well as domestic affairs.

The question for a political community such as Scotland ambitious for more self-determination in an interdependent world is how far independence would secure a net increase in its own and the wider global welfare. That question can only be answered in the particular but OECD statistics illuminate the scope for difference that still exists for developed states in the most integrated region of the globe. For example, general government revenues as a share of GDP range from 55% in Denmark to 35% in Ireland, government social expenditure ranges from 29% GDP in Sweden and France to 16% in Ireland, taxes on income and profits from 29% in Denmark to 10% in Ireland and the Netherlands, tax on the average worker from 52% in Germany and 49% in France to 22% in Ireland and 32% in the UK, public pensions expenditure from 5% in Denmark to 12% in Finland and 11% in Germany (OECD, 2010).[13]

Some on the Left will complain that these are minor variations on a common capitalist theme while those on the Right may claim – mistakenly as the OECD's annual series makes clear – that they conceal an irresistible trend towards a shrinking role for the state. But the variations are not trivial: they play a large part in determining the differences in levels of public services, poverty and inequality or competitiveness between countries and take their place alongside differences on such issues as the balance between fossil fuels and renewables, the level of public ownership of the economy, the role of trade unions and mutuals, social and economic inequality, and the extent of state support for the arts – all reflecting the deliberately chosen political preferences of voters.

Another proximate measure of the scope for difference lies in the range of international affiliations among the small countries of western Europe. Switzerland remains outwith the EU and the European Economic Area (EEA) but within the European Free Trade Area (EFTA); Norway is outwith the EU but is a member of EFTA and the EEA and is a non-nuclear member of NATO; Denmark is a member of the EU but with an opt-out from the eurozone and is a non-nuclear member of NATO; Sweden is a member of the EU but not of the eurozone or of NATO; Finland, Austria and Ireland are members of the EU and the eurozone but not of NATO; Iceland is a member of the EEA and EFTA but not of the EU or NATO; the Faroes and Greenland have home rule within a continuing foreign policy relationship with Denmark but are outwith the EU; the Benelux countries are ensconced at the very heart of the EU's integration project although, partly as a result, Belgium is facing separatist challenges to its very existence.

The diversity of these institutional relationships is repeated in the positions taken on foreign policy issues – on the invasion of Iraq, the UN/NATO intervention in Afghanistan, international development aid, climate change, the NATO intervention in Libya, the Palestinian Authority's bid for membership of the UN and UNESCO, an international tax on financial transactions, attitudes to nuclear weapons and many more.

The lesson Scots should take from this diversity is to choose the political status which maximises their own welfare and their capacity to contribute to the wider international good, acknowledging such constraints as appear significant within their environment but without too much regard for theories of what is or is not possible. They should be guided by their particular circumstances, not by principles of global interdependence postulated by academic researchers. They need to assess what the right conferred by independence to speak for themselves in joint if unequal international governance structures would be worth in practice. At issue is the freedom of a political community to decide its own priorities, to advocate them in international forums, and then, depending on the outcome, to make its own judgement on what accommodation to make with others' judgements of the 'imperatives' of interdependence. Such freedom is exercised by numerous members of the international community with populations comparable to or smaller than Scotland's.

There is no block on Scotland's ambitions to take democratic control over her future except from the judgements the people of Scotland make of where their best interest lies.

Independence and Democracy

By ensuring that Scottish voters consistently got the governments they voted for without having to endure long periods of governments they had voted against, independence would correct the most egregious of the components of Scotland's democratic deficit. And by definition the government functions over which their democratic preferences would apply would extend to the full range of powers possessed by independent states including tax and benefits, defence and foreign affairs.

What is more, the policy preferences of Scottish voters would not be subject to the gross distortions caused by Westminster's first-past-the-post voting system. In developing its proposals for legislative devolution to Scotland, the Labour Party understood that the Westminster system of which it was a major beneficiary would not be acceptable to Scottish opinion for the new Scottish Parliament. So it proposed a combination of the first-past-the-post system arid a regional topping-up or list system to correct the more conspicuous distortions of first-past-the-post. While not a fully proportional system, it was a major rebuke to Westminster's disdain for the most basic requirement of representative government: that the composition of the legislature should accurately reflect the views of the electorate.

The Scottish dynamic for a more democratic form of government was displayed again when the Scottish Parliament legislated in 2003 for the single transferable vote (STV), the purest form of proportional representation, for local government elections in Scotland.

While the Scotland Act of 1998 perversely reserved to Westminster the power to change the electoral system for the Parliament, it devolved the power to change the voting system for local government. In a Parliament deliberately biased towards multiparty government the price of Liberal Democrat support for Labour to form the first Scottish Executive (1999–2003) was that the full STV package rejected by Westminster for the Parliament be implemented for Scottish local government. As anticipated, at the local elections in 2007 the new voting system destroyed Labour's domination of Scottish local government, which it had traditionally enjoyed on a minority share of the Scottish vote.

Scotland Falls Short

But the improvements on the Westminster model fall far short of establishing Scotland as the model of a vigorous popular democracy. The turnout for general elections in devolved Scotland has been lower by 7–15% than the UK wide turn out for the nearest UK general elections and lower than the Scottish turnout for UK elections by 8–12% (UK Political Info website, 2011).[14] After 10 years of devolution, decision-taking remains highly centralised with local authorities enjoying only marginally more spending discretion than in the rest of the UK and rather less fiscal autonomy after a four year freeze of council taxes, now extended for a fifth year. While Scottish civil society has grown in size and vigour in response to political devolution there is no evidence of a higher level of popular participation in politics than in the UK as a whole. Meanwhile the share of seats in the Scottish Parliament held by women has been on a declining trend from a modest 39.5% in 1999 to 34.8% in 2011 (Mackay and Kenny, 2011).[15]

While independence would correct the structural deficits of Scottish democracy, there is no guarantee that it would revive the democratic dynamic of the first phase of devolution. But it would certainly open up new opportunities. Whatever route Scotland takes to achieve independence, it will need to be entrenched in a constitution. It is inconceivable that a Scottish constitution would ignore current concerns within the UK as a whole about the centralisation of power, the failures of parliamentary scrutiny and accountability shown by such decisions as the invasion of Iraq on doctored evidence, the erosion of classic liberties and the low level of popular participation in democratic politics. The explicit replacement in a Scottish constitution of the English doctrine of parliamentary sovereignty by the Scottish doctrine of popular sovereignty as the source of political authority would open the door to more radical versions of popular democracy than Westminster politics are ever likely to accommodate. We could expect that a Scottish constitution would not only entrench the good features of the devolution settlement such as fixed-term parliaments, and at the very least examine how to strengthen some of the underperforming features such as the committee system and the petitions system but go beyond these to consider constitutional reinforcement to the rights of local government and of local communities, define a voter's right of popular initiative and perhaps of recall, and clarify the rights of users of public services. The need to draft and agree a Scottish constitution would itself be an opportunity for a major public debate about the future of Scottish democracy, culminating in a referendum (Bulmer, 2011).[16]

The Quality of Democracy

The quality of a nation's democratic life cannot just be inferred from formal characteristics such as its political status, its voting system and other provisions of its constitution. It depends as much on the tenor and vigour of its public culture. The Republic of Ireland has an irreproachably democratic constitution but also an unenviable record of political corruption (O'Toole, 2009).[17] While devolved Scotland has been free of corruption on the Irish scale, it has other serious weaknesses, among them a low level of public participation and an enfeebled media, as well as a relatively low intellectual input from Scottish universities, think tanks and other institutions of Scottish civil society. How far these weaknesses can be attributed to Scotland's subordinate political status, how far they are endemic to Scottish culture or to Scotland's position in English-speaking global communications and cultural networks, are important questions in the debate on Scotland's political future.

Against expectation, the mainstream Scottish print and broadcast media have been in retreat over the devolution decade. The two Scottish-produced quality papers, *The Herald* and *The Scotsman*, saw their circulation cut by half between 2000 and 2011, to 48,000 and 40,000 respectively. Their Sunday stablemates, the *Sunday Herald* and *Scotland on Sunday* – on their respective launches in 1988 and 1999 hailed as evidence of the Scottish press gearing itself up for a new devolutionary phase of Scottish politics – suffered even greater losses to *c.* 38,000 and 29,610 by November 2011 (Audit Bureau of Circulation, 2011).[18] What modest enhancement of political coverage has occurred in the mainstream media in response to the establishment of the Scottish Parliament has usually been restricted to more talking heads in off-peak slots with investigative and analytical programmes still at a premium. Scotland's premier daily current affairs programme *Good Morning Scotland* struggles to keep ahead of Radio 4's *Today* in Scottish affections. One bright spot in BBC Scotland's output has been the growth of an audience for the Gaelic language channel BBC Alba which, through its *Eorpa* series, has demonstrated more consistent curiosity about the rest of the world than BBC Scotland. There are some encouraging signs too for STV's revival. On the other hand, despite a plethora of small websites discussing national issues, most of them individual political blogs, Scotland has failed to develop a significant online forum for public debate comparable in its reach or quality of content to open democracy.net or the *Guardian*'s Comment Is Free forum.

The one sector where devolution has stimulated a positive if still modest response is civil society. From a low level pre-devolution, the Scottish universities have over recent years established several public policy networks with the aim of making their academic expertise available to the wider Scottish policy community in government and the third sector. A number of specialist research units, among them the Fraser of Allander Institute on the Scottish Economy at Strathclyde University, the Centre for Public Policy for the Regions at Glasgow University and the Institute for the Study of Scottish Government and the Centre for Social Research at Edinburgh University, now regularly inform the Scottish debate. The voluntary sector too has responded positively, by increasing its lobbying capacity several fold – though, with some exceptions, notably on the environment and on social care, its capacity and perhaps its ambition to lead policy debate has lagged behind. Independent think tanks remain rare on the Scottish scene with the Scottish Council Foundation having closed with the first devolution decade leaving only a single successor of substance in Reform Scotland alongside the Scottish Futures Forum established by the Scottish Parliament.

Advocates of independence might argue that some of the stimulus expected from devolution has been undercut by the Scottish public's awareness of the strict limitations imposed by the devolution settlement on the powers of the Scottish Parliament and that independence, or even 'devo max', would deliver an altogether stronger stimulus to Scotland's democratic culture and infrastructure. And they could cite the higher level of public participation and the more robust national media of most of the small independent European democracies in support.

However it cannot be assumed that the quality of democracy in an independent Scotland would evolve naturally to match the quality of the most developed European democracies. In addition to obvious differences between the social and cultural legacies of Scotland and the Nordic countries, for example, the reinvigoration of democracy confronts powerful contemporary trends. These include greater individualism, the erosion of traditional 'solidary' organisations such as trade unions and churches, not to mention political parties themselves, the diversification and fragmentation of mass communication, and the concentration and growing influence of corporate power. The same trends, of course, handicap the progress of any independence movement, or indeed any movement of reform or transformation which depends on wide democratic mobilisation. It is this tension which gives the independence movement in Scotland, like its counterparts in Québec and Catalonia, its wider political and cultural significance. While the global economic and political environment is generally sympathetic to the claims of small societies to statehood it is less sympathetic to their prospects for their developing a self-determining culture to support their political ambitions.

The claim that independence would lead to a reinvigoration of Scotland's public culture faces a particular British obstacle. Independence would not insulate Scotland against the dominance of London. The mainstream case for Scottish independence looks forward to Scotland being in an economic and social union with the UK and to continuing the current close collaboration between academic and cultural institutions north and south of the border. While the extension and consolidation of Scotland's political institutions and civil society which would accompany independence will strengthen Scotland's public culture, English influence supported by a shared language and amplified by London's status as the UK's sole 'global city' will continue to be formidable. In 2005 – before the banking crisis and economic downturn and before the BBC's decentralisation to Salford – London, with just 12% of the UK's population, provided 54% of the UK's TV and radio workforce and London and the South East together provided 57% of Britain's creative workforce (GLA Economics, 2008).[19] The bare workforce statistics do not capture the real balance of media and cultural power in London's favour which draws on a vast inheritance of cultural assets from all over the UK and beyond, an overwhelming predominance of the top media and cultural decision takers, and a highly favourable distribution of public cultural spending as well as of private patronage, much of it tax privileged. While the economic downturn is likely to have reduced the economic base of London's media and cultural sectors, there is nothing to suggest that their relative power within the UK has diminished. Indeed, given the greater economic resilience of London and the south-east in the financial crisis, their role is as likely to have been enhanced as diminished.

The challenge for an independent Scotland will be to find sufficient space under this heavy carapace of London influence to establish the institutions which could support a reinvigorated Scottish democracy: a stronger Scottish print and broadcast media and internet presence; more Scottish think tanks; Scottish universities making a stronger contribution to Scottish policy debates; and the strengthening of existing national cultural institutions along with the promotion of local and community arts organisations. Scotland's third sector will need ambition and capacity to lead Scottish opinion (Sime, 2011).[20] Some of these developments might come from civil society as a spontaneous response to the stimulus of independence but others would need public intervention and funding to challenge the wider global trends described above.

Conclusion

The democratic case for independence rests on two irrefutable claims – that it would guarantee that the government of Scotland was aligned with the preferences of the Scottish voter, and that the reach of Scottish democratic decision-taking was equal to that of other independent countries; and two plausible claims – that by distancing Scotland from the conservatism of British political culture it would create new opportunities to extend democracy in Scotland and lead to a strengthening of the civil institutions and public culture necessary to sustain a vigorous democratic culture.

References

1 Commission on Scottish Devolution, *Serving Scotland Better: Scotland and the United Kingdom in the 21st Century*. HMG, 2009.

2 Keegan, W, *Britain Without Oil*. London, 1983.

3 Independent Budget Report. Scottish Government, Edinburgh, 2010.

4 NSD European Election Database website: EU related referendums 1972–2009.

5 Democracy Index 2010. *Economist* Intelligence Unit, London, 2010.

6 *Choosing Scotland's Future*. Scottish Government, Edinburgh, 2007.

7 Scottish Social Attitudes Survey 2010: Attitudes to Government, the Economy and Public Services in Scotland. Scottish Government, 2011.

8 Commission on Scottish Devolution, 2009.

9 Scottish Government, 2010.

10 Government Expenditure and Revenue in Scotland reports 2004–10. Scottish Government, Edinburgh, 2005–12.

11 Davies, R, *Devolution: A Process Not an Event*. Institute of Welsh Affairs, Cardiff, 1999.

12 Keating M, *The Independence of Scotland*. Oxford University Press, 2009; letter to *The Guardian*, 29/05/2011.

13 OECD Country reports website, 2008 figures; 2010 edition.

14 *General Election Turnout Since 1945, by Region*. UK Political Info website 2011.

15 Mackay, F and Kenny, M, 'In the Balance: Women and the 2011 Scottish Parliament Elections'. *Scottish Affairs* No. 76, Summer 2011.

16 Bulmer, E, *A Model Constitution for Scotland: Making Democracy Work in an Independent State*, Edinburgh, 2011.

17 O'Toole, F, *Ship of Fools*. London, 2009.

18 Audit Bureau of Circulation, 2011.

19 *London: A Cultural Audit,* GLA Economics, 2008.

20 Sime, M, *The Scotsman*, 16/12/2011.

The Economic Case

Introduction

SCOTLAND'S SUBORDINATE POLITICAL STATUS within the UK relegates Scotland's needs and opportunities to a secondary status in UK policy making, frustrates Scottish initiative, and obstructs the full development of Scotland's sense of responsibility for its own welfare and for its contribution to global welfare. These effects can be illustrated with particular clarity in economic policy.

Claims and counterclaims about the effects of independence on the Scottish economy have been the staple of the independence debate since the emergence of the SNP as a significant political force in the 1960s. Initially, the onus was on the advocates of independence to demonstrate that independence was economically viable. The most frequent challenges were over how Scotland could secure her main export market in England in the event of independence, and whether she would be able to pay for the welfare state built up in the first postwar decades. The reassurances which Nationalists were able to offer then may have been economically valid but they were too complex for the embryonic public debate.

Oil Economics

When oil in commercially attractive quantities was discovered in the Scottish province of the North Sea at the end of the sixties, the onus shifted to the opponents of independence to demonstrate why an independent Scotland with control over the oil would *not* be better off. That this was not just a Nationalist conceit was confirmed in *The Economics of Nationalism Re-examined* by the chief Economic Adviser to the Scottish Office (McCrone, 1975).[1] McCrone's paper, which concluded that 'the advent of North Sea oil has completely overturned the traditional economic argument used against Scottish nationalism', was circulated only to a small number of senior politicians and civil servants and was not made public until 2005.

While the volumes and timetables of McCrone's analysis need to be adjusted, the fundamentals still apply: despite 40 billion barrels of oil having been extracted from the Scottish oil province since 1975, 21–35 billion barrels of recoverable oil remain, with prices expected to follow an upward trend (Kemp, 2011).[2] Scotland's green energy potential strengthens her longer-term economic prospects. Today, as for the past three decades, the question is not whether Scotland would be viable as an independent country but whether it would be significantly better off.

There is no simple answer to that question. Economics cannot make confident predictions of the future: there are simply too many variables – political, social, environmental, technological – to support a high level of confidence in economic predictions. As a result the debate has tended to converge on what appears to be the more solid ground of the conventional economic data available in official reports and academic analyses.

Flawed Data

Unfortunately such data are themselves flawed as a basis for assessing the prospects for an economy. The most frequently cited data source in the debate on independence is the annual report *Government Revenue and Expenditure in Scotland* (GERS) published by the Scottish Government. This sets out to provide as accurate a picture as possible of Government income and expenditure in Scotland. But its estimates depend on figures which are usually two years old and which each year carry a warning about their accuracy.

It should also carry a warning against reading off from the figures the budgetary balance of an independent Scotland. GERS provides estimates of Government revenue from and expenditure on Scotland *as part of the* UK, including expenditure by the UK Government on behalf of Scotland but spent outside Scotland. Such retained UK expenditure, which constitutes 30% of the Scottish total, includes some high cost items such as defence expenditure, including expenditure on the UK's nuclear deterrent and the Iraq war which an independent Scotland would have been unlikely to have supported, as well as costs such as the London Olympics and the House of Lords which an independent Scotland would not incur. Savings in these areas alone would be around £200m a year. There are also problems with its revenue estimates, particularly of company taxation and of personal taxes paid by resident Scots working in other parts of the UK.

For many years, GERS presented its conclusions on the net fiscal balance for Scotland without providing a comparison with the UK balance. This meant that Scotland was presented as being in deficit without the corresponding figures for the UK's net balance which more often than not would have shown the UK also to be in deficit. From 2008–09 GERS has repaired this omission, so ensuring that if UK national debt rises as expected over the next several years the impact on both the UK and Scottish fiscal balances will be identified. GERS 2004–05 to 2008–09 showed Scotland with its share of North Sea oil revenues running a modest surplus on its current balance while in deficit on its overall fiscal balance but at a lower level than the UK which was in deficit on both its current and its net balance (Scottish Government, 2011).[3]

Dynamic Effects

The most significant limitation of GERS as a source of evidence in the debate on the economic effects of independence is that it necessarily provides a static analysis of Scotland's fiscal position. This ignores the core of the case for independence, that by providing a government directly responsive to Scottish needs and opportunities, and informed by a more sophisticated public debate, independence would improve the dynamics of the Scottish economy and thus its fiscal and broader economic prospects.

In assessing how reasonable it is to expect a dynamic effect on the Scottish economy from independence, we need to appeal to a much broader range of evidence than the income and expenditure estimates provided by reports such as GERS. This will include the insights of historians and political economists into the relationship between the constitutional powers and institutional capacities of states and their economic and social health as well as more conventional economic analyses.

An initial appeal can be made to popular maxims, those generalisations from experience which frame so much political debate. The adage that democracy is the worst system of government except for all the others applies equally to independence. The government of any people is best provided by the people themselves. Who else is as well qualified to know their needs and best opportunities? Certainly not distant others, particularly if the political culture and the economic and social conditions in which they habitually operate as politicians are significantly different.

As for individuals, so for nations. Independence is the status most likely to promote initiative and a robust sense of self-responsibility. Institutionalised dependence on others to take the key decisions encourages fatalism and cynicism in groups as well as in individuals. Distant others will always give priority to the needs and conventions of their own society, even where the population balance is more equal than it is in the UK: meanwhile they do us the disservice of providing easy alibis for our own inertia.

Because the most valuable of all economic assets is applied human intelligence, a system of government should encourage as many people as possible to share in decisions. Distant decision-taking obstructs participation and encourages the most ambitious members of the community, who will usually include a disproportionate share of the most able, to emigrate to other centres of power. By extending the range of public careers in Scotland and the satisfaction to be had from them, independence would improve the incentive for the most able Scots to remain in Scotland so raising the quality of public debate and decision taking. Since the start of the devolved Scottish Parliament too many leading Scottish politicians from the Unionist parties have side-stepped Holyrood to keep open their chances of climbing Westminster's higher and greasier pole. No doubt there will always be Scots who, either because of ambition or because they identify themselves as British, will want to pursue public careers in England. But the greater opportunities and the higher stakes offered by an independent Scotland would help to limit the flow of political talent to the south.

Many of the most critical decisions in economic policy are about the balance to be struck between current consumption and investment for the future. The people most likely to strike the right balance between the needs of present and future generations in a community are those committed to living and bringing up their families there. A society whose rulers spend most of their time in a distant metropolis, especially one as preoccupied with its own interests as a 'global city' as London, has only itself to blame if it finds its needs treated as secondary to those of the metropolis.

If independence encourages a greater sense of responsibility in voters for their own futures, it will increase the incentives for greater efficiency in the allocation of public money – an argument that should carry a particular appeal to those who maintain that Scotland has a chronic dependency on subsidies from England. No longer would Scottish politicians be able to avoid tough spending decisions by raising a clamour for the London Treasury to direct more of its spending north of the border.

It would be absurd to accept such political folk-wisdom as settling the matter. As high-level generalisations, maxims come with any number of conditions and qualifications and can seldom claim validation by an Economic and Social Research Council research programme. Yet it would be equally foolish to dismiss them simply as old wives' tales. Following the banking crisis, we have got used to hearing from economists that 'banks which are too big to fail are bad banks'. Whether they concern banks or nations, such general truths carry a strong provisional authority. If the opponents of independence have a more persuasive set of maxims or academic studies, let us hear them.

Displacement Effect

Independence would also eliminate the attention displacement effect demonstrated time and again by Scotland's elected representatives at Westminster. During the 1970s the SNP's 'It's Scotland's Oil' campaign forced the Unionist parties to give some attention to the implications of oil developments for the Scottish economy. To be sure, most of that attention took the form of polemical denials of the SNP's claim that with Scottish control the oil could transform Scotland's economic prospects. But by the end of the 1970s, in response to public sentiment that Scotland should have a degree of privileged access to the oil revenues, the Labour Party grudgingly conceded the principle of a Scottish oil fund. That was about as far as Unionist interest in the Scottish potential of the oil went in public, though Government papers released in 2009 under the '30-year rule' and unearthed by investigative journalist

George Rosie revealed that senior Ministers and Whitehall officials were well aware of the importance of North Sea oil to the UK's international creditworthiness as it attempted to recover from the 1976 sterling crisis and subsequent IMF deflation (HM Treasury, 1975).[4] But following the SNP's reverse in the 1979 election, the interest of Scotland's Labour MPs in the Scottish dimension of North Sea oil drained away. This left Mrs Thatcher to enjoy the benefits of £160bn of oil revenues (2008 prices) undisturbed by any concerted challenge from Scotland's majority Labour MPs, many representing constituencies being devastated by her Government's policies.

In the run-up to the banking crisis, three Scottish MPs occupied critical positions in the UK's political structure – Gordon Brown as Chancellor and then Prime Minister, Alistair Darling as Chief Secretary to the Treasury and then Chancellor, and John McFall as Chair of the Commons' Treasury Select Committee. Despite their respective responsibilities for supervising and regulating the UK's banks, none of the three appears to have had any thought for the implications for the Scottish economy of the runaway expansion of the two biggest Scottish banks, not even Alistair Darling as an MP for Edinburgh, the centre of Scottish banking.

Even when the crisis finally broke in October 2008, the three had little to say about the Scottish dimension. Each of them dismissed Scottish pleas that Lloyds' takeover of HBOS be referred to the Competition Commission. Perhaps even more extraordinary, two years after the crisis neither Brown nor Darling had expressed any views on the prospects or options for rebuilding a Scottish-based banking sector. As late as May 2011, the extent of Darling's thoughts on the future of Scottish banking was a concern that when the public equity in the Royal Bank of Scotland was sold off, the bank's headquarters should remain in Edinburgh. The bank's ownership, its structure and governance were ignored as were the needs of Scotland's economy for a more diversified banking system (Darling, 2011).[5] His memoir of his time as Chancellor of the Exchequer continues that indifference (Darling, 2011).[6] In the biggest crisis for the Scottish economy in six decades, these three senior Scottish MPs have had nothing of significance to say about the future of a Scottish banking sector brought to collapse under their stewardship.

The most topical example of this displacement effect is Scottish politicians' response to the new Coalition Government's strategy for reducing the UK's budget deficit. Scottish MPs and MSPs knew that Scotland was one of the regions of the UK most vulnerable to a short-term strategy for eliminating the deficit focused on cuts to public expenditure. They had no excuse for not knowing that from 2004–05 to 2008–09, according to GERS, Scotland's current budget was in surplus and that while it moved into deficit in 2009–10, that deficit was still smaller as a share of GDP than the UK deficit. They knew, or ought to have known, that one of the most serious obstacles to Scotland transforming itself into a major producer and net exporter of green energy alongside oil is the planned 36% cut in real terms to Scotland's capital budget, and that the traditional way of overcoming a scarcity of development capital is to borrow in international markets using future revenues as security, as Norway and the UK both did in the development phases of their oil industries.

Against these presumptions, Scotland's Unionist MPs have shown no sign that they recognise any divergence between UK and Scottish needs. The leading Scottish Liberal Democrats in the coalition, Treasury Secretary Danny Alexander and Scottish Secretary Michael Moore, have demonstrated no more tolerance for arguments for Scottish budgetary exceptionalism than for criticism of Calman's inept taxation proposals, while Scotland's Labour MPs have adopted their traditional three monkeys' response to any suggestion of a Scottish alternative that might offer their long-suffering constituents some hope of escaping the latest assault by a Westminster slash-and-burn Government. Where a nation's political leaders are so persistently careless of its best opportunities for development, hopes for a more prosperous and fulfilling future are chaff in the wind.

It is possible that the Unionists' display of indifference to Scotland's changing prospects conceals a sequence of conscientiously informed judgements which invariably find that whatever the circumstances, Scotland's interest is best served by hanging on to Britannia. But as Scotland's Unionists are conspicuously reluctant to engage with the strategic case for independence, that must remain a matter of speculation. The more plausible explanation is that Scotland's subordinate status in the UK supports a distribution of political career opportunities which disposes too many of the most politically ambitious Scots simply to dismiss Scotland's distinctive needs and opportunties.

Globalisation as Solvent

One feature of globalisation largely neglected in Unionist discourse about independence is that it works to dissolve unions as much as to obstruct independence. This solvent effect used to appear most frequently in the form of decolonisation. Today its roots go wider. When a metropolitan state is unable to control the impact of external forces on its regions they will begin to feel the need for greater power to act in their own defence. The more confident among them will naturally look to examples of similarly sized and positioned political communities with a superior record of economic and social development. And many of these will be found within federal or independent states.

Ironically, the logic of this process is most evident in London, a city which has probably done more over the centuries to promote globalisation than any other. Its role has depended on its long history as a national capital, first of England and then of Great Britain in its imperial heyday, attracting massive political, economic and cultural investment from the rest of the UK in a process that continues today. No wonder that prior to the banking crisis the London Development Agency had the confidence to summarise London's role as 'a centre for the location of advanced producer services, a centre of command and control for government and multinational corporations, a connecting node in the world networks established by trade and industry' (London Development Agency, 2006).[7] Even after the UK taxpayer rescued London's banking sector, London's promotional efforts on behalf of its future as a global city have continued unabated, boosted by such events as the Olympics, and royal weddings and jubilees.

Scotland has been particularly exposed to the consequences of London's leading role in globalisation. As the junior partner in the British empire she was both beneficiary and victim: beneficiary from the new opportunities provided for the accumulation of wealth through trade and manufacture and the expansion of new career opportunities; victim from the intensity of industrialisation and the high human cost of Scotland's contribution to the military needs of the empire. In the post-war period the cost was paid not just in the hectic rate of Scotland's de-industrialisation but also in the increasing focus of British policy making on the needs of London's financial sector. Just when the massive oil revenues flowing into the HM Treasury in the late 1970s and early 1980s were providing the means to recapitalise the economy, the voters of England handed power over to a generation of Conservative politicians who were more interested in shrinking the state – and the unions – and in making the EU a safe market for London's financial sector through the single internal market than in restoring the manufacturing sector or the public infrastructure of the UK. As a result the centralisation of economic and political power was massively reinforced, a process which in the opinion of some analysts is being repeated in the aftermath of the banking crisis (Ertuk et al., 2011).[8]

Institutions

In addition to establishing new foci of political attention, independence would require the development of the range of public institutions which other developed, independent countries have found they need to flourish in a complex, interdependent world. The quality of a country's policy-making depends in part on its collective memory. And that memory depends in part on public bureaucracies.

Before the neo-liberals howl that this would mean an even more bloated public sector in Scotland consider how Scotland might have benefited in the run-up to the banking crisis from the experience of prudential banking regulation accumulated by the core Nordic countries (OECD, Norway, 2010).[9] Despite the scale and European profile of Scotland's financial sector before the credit crunch, Scotland had little expertise, either within Government or outside it, to draw on in anticipating the crisis or in developing its response. Scotland has had no formal voice in UK financial regulation – no representation on the Board of the Bank of England, the Monetary Policy Committee or the Financial Services Authority – and no dedicated supervisory agency of its own (Scottish Parliament, 2010).[10] Nor does the system of financial regulation proposed by the Coalition Government make any provision for Scottish representation. The Competition Commission usually has some members of Scottish background or connections but again with no designated responsibility to consult with or report back to the Scottish Government or Parliament.

Nor are finance and competition the only areas in which UK regulation has failed Scotland. The UK's energy regulator, Ofgem, failed for years to take the most basic action to protect low income Scots families with their higher heating bills against the threat of fuel poverty and it continues to drag its feet on the high transmission charges facing Scottish energy producers on the National Grid. The broadcasting regulators, Ofcom, and the BBC have often turned a tin ear to the complaints of audiences in Scotland – for example, on the inability of large areas of the southern Borders and Dumfries and Galloway to access Scottish television programmes and the discriminatory treatment of Scotland on the issue of the leaders' debates in the 2010 UK General Election, not to mention the inaction of the UK Government and broadcasters to the wider issues raised by the Scottish Broadcasting Commission's 2008 proposal for a Scottish Digital Network.[11]

The lack of a hinterland of public institutions capable of supporting and guiding Scottish policy making goes beyond these failures of the UK's regulatory agencies, serious though they have been for Scotland. By comparison with the Nordic countries, the infrastructure of public institutions supporting the development of public policy in Scotland remains threadbare. Although the 1998 devolution settlement gave Scotland responsibility for economic development, energy and industry were reserved to Westminster. No surprise, then, that Scottish Governments have had neither the incentive nor the resources to create a Scottish equivalent of Norway's Petroleum Directorate, established in 1972 within the Ministry of Petroleum and Energy (1978) to advise on energy policy and to diversify the Norwegian energy industry's links around the world. Despite the size of Scotland's energy sector, not to mention the scale of Scotland's energy ambitions, the Scottish Government's Energy Division employs 60 people, many of them on routine consents work (2011 figures), just half the complement of the Petroleum Directorate which is one component of Norway's Ministry of Energy. Equally Scotland might envy Finland's ecology of industrial innovation built around such organisations as the not-for-profit joint public and private agency VTT, founded 60 years ago; today northern Europe's largest applied research organisation, VTT, with a workforce of 2,700, promotes product and systems innovation for the public and private sectors. And Scotland might have learned from the models of more open policy development as exemplified by Sweden's semi-autonomous public agencies and their wide use of academic and other expertise (Oxford Economics, 2011).[12] Only with the coming of devolution, though not solely because of it, have Scotland's public bureaucracies begun to diverge from the more closed Whitehall models.

Taken together, these omissions and contrasts signal that Scotland is operating without the levels of experience and expertise which other small developed countries have built up within their public bureaucracies. Why does that matter when under devolution the experience and expertise of the UK government is available to it? Because a country exposed simultaneously to the challenges of globalisation and a growing divergence between its own economic opportunities and policy preferences and those of its metropolitan centre needs to be able to articulate its options directly and authoritatively to its international and domestic partners and audiences. To do that it needs the appropriate institutions. Under devo max or full independence, the creation of such institutional capacities would not only make the Scottish state a better informed and more effective agent of Scottish interests but also help to create a more educated public culture in Scotland.

International Comparisons

The conventional economic case for independence draws on two main categories of evidence – comparative data on Scotland's economic performance relative to the UK and to other comparable European states and specific instances of where Scotland's economic interest has been damaged by membership of the UK.

Between 1977 and 2007, Scotland's average GDP growth at 1.9% lagged behind a selection of its most obvious European comparators, including the UK, by 0.1–3.1% annually, compared to Ireland's 5.4%, Iceland's 3.4%, Norway's 3.1%, Denmark's 2.0%, Finland's 2.9%, Sweden's 2.3% and the 2.4% of Austria and the UK (Scottish Government, 2009).[13]

While such data suggest that Scotland within the UK is failing to achieve its economic potential, they do not prove it. Perhaps Scotland's potential for growth is actually lower than that of the UK and other Western European countries. In support of Scotland's potential, champions of independence can cite such factors as its relatively high educational standards, the disproportionate contribution of its universities to cited scientific research publications, its wealth of energy resources, and its stable and relatively well developed government and civil society. Their opponents can cite its burden of poor health, the high level of external ownership of its economy, its poor entrepreneurial record over the last century or, for the most pessimistic, a chronic lack of political confidence.

The bare contrast which Nationalists draw between Scotland's economic performance and the performance of their favourite comparators – Norway, Finland, Denmark and Sweden along with Ireland – refutes any claim that small countries cannot hope to achieve economic success. But it does not establish that independence is a condition of their success, even less that an independent Scotland could emulate it. The argument that Scotland has been performing below what might reasonably be expected given her overall circumstances is not open to statistical demonstration. The evidence is circumstantial and contestable. If the argument persuades it does so because in the end it combines to form a more plausible representation of the opportunities and risks than the opposing case that the best future Scotland can hope for lies within the UK.

The Nordic Record: Denmark

The modern histories of the Nordic countries, as of western Europe's other small democracies, reveal a record of successful adaptation to often daunting changes in their circumstances, suggesting that small states, more particularly small democracies, possess an impressive resilience.

For much of the 19th century, Denmark struggled with the economic and political consequences of being on the losing side of the Napoleonic Wars, most obviously through the loss of Norway to Sweden. Then in the middle of the century, shortly after its mainly grain-producing economy had recovered from the effects of the wars, it was faced with the challenge of new competition from the grain farmers of the Americas and Russia, who were using the expanding railways to bring their grain to Europe's growing urban markets. In the 1880s alone, 77,000 Danes emigrated to the US. But over the next 50 years, Denmark switched the base of its agriculture from grain to dairy and meat production: by 1900, dairy and meat products contributed around 70%

of a total agricultural output which had grown overall by 400%. The transformation was facilitated by land reforms but owed much of its success to the educational programme of the Danish Folk High School movement inspired by the romantic Danish nationalist Nils Grundtvig and to the rapid spread of cooperative ideas from Britain.

This was just one of the economic transformations which modern Denmark has successfully undertaken. The inter-war depression caused massive unemployment, up to 40% in some industrial areas, and widespread poverty on a scale which exceeded the levels in Scotland. The Danish Prime Minister of the day estimated that about 50% of the population had no purchasing power. In 1933 the mounting crisis forced ideological rivals the Social Democrats and the liberals (the Venstre) to collaborate in negotiating the Kanslergade Agreement, embracing Keynesian deficit financing, exchange controls and a package of social reforms which laid the grounds for the future Danish welfare state. Within this framework Denmark was able to continue its rapid adaptation to a manufacturing economy. In 1930, 50% of the workforce was still agricultural: on the eve of the Second World War that had declined to 33%. An extension of this 'Danish model' supported Denmark's continued evolution after the Second World War towards a technology- and service-based economy increasingly integrated with the international economy and enjoying a steady if unspectacular 2.5% annual growth rate 1975–2005 (Jespersen, 2007).[14]

Sweden

Sweden shared Denmark's need to undertake a radical readjustment of its economy in its decline from its imperial role in the 17th century. While it had a greater diversity of natural resources, extending from agriculture to timber and minerals (principally copper and iron ore), it was handicapped by a social conservatism which slowed both its political and economic development. Sweden's first phase of industrialisation, from the 1850s, was based on the processing of mineral deposits and timber, mainly for export. While these early developments took place principally in the countryside where the bulk of Sweden's population lived, the application of electricity, an increasing proportion of which was hydro generated, encouraged a move to greater concentration in urban areas.

While the progress of industrialisation in Sweden was more gradual than in Scotland and its impact less traumatic, Swedish politics were fully exposed to the turmoil of the economic changes. Between 1840 and 1910, an estimated one million Swedes emigrated, mainly to North America. Despite the benefits of neutrality in the First World War, the inter-war depression hit Sweden hard: unemployment reached nearly 30%, provoking a rise in labour militancy and sometimes violent strike action and the currency was devalued by 30%. The political response was led by the rapidly emerging Social Democrats with their concept of a Swedish 'Folkhem' or 'People's Home'. With a major contribution from Sweden's enlightened bureaucrats and progressive academics such as the social anthropologists Gunnar and Alva Myrdal, the Social Democratic model was formalised in the Saltsjöbaden Agreement of 1938, based on a privately owned economy subject to a high level of regulation, a managed labour market in which the trade unions were leading partners, and a comprehensive welfare state supported by high levels of taxation. Despite the economic and political turbulence, many of the Swedish technology and engineering companies, including Volvo, SAAB and Ericsson which flourished in the second half of the century, were founded in this period (Kent, 2008).[15]

The Swedish model came under serious challenge in the 1970s when the rise in oil prices exacerbated its inherent inflationary tendency, leading to a devaluation of the krona. Reforms to adapt the model to the more challenging external environment were pulled into the wider movement for privatisation and for deregulation of the financial industry led by the UK under Mrs Thatcher. A credit-led property boom followed. The bursting of the bubble in 1990 led to a 5% loss of GDP, a 10% drop in employment, and a budget deficit of 13% of GDP in 1993. The Government assumed responsibility for 25% of the country's banking assets at a cost of 4% of national wealth. It took until 1998 for the national budget to return to surplus and interest rates to converge on the euro rates. The global banking crisis of 2008 caused another 5% loss of GDP and a rise to 9.3% unemployment, but under a new centre-right Government growth of 3% was forecast for 2011–14.

Finland

While the modern histories of Denmark and Sweden contain their fair measure of political *Sturm und Drang,* they were outperformed by Norway and Finland. At the beginning of the 18th century, Norway and Finland were, politically and economically, the least developed of the core Nordic countries. For much of their modern history, they were subject to the rule of one or other of the great powers of northern Europe. Norway was ruled by Denmark until 1815 and then handed over to Sweden, with a significant degree of internal home rule under the 1814 Eidsvoll constitution, until it finally asserted its independence in 1905. Finland was a province of Sweden until 1809 when it was transferred to Russian control with the status of a Grand Duchy, enjoying a substantial but politically precarious measure of internal control.

For most of the 19th century, the Finnish economy was based on fishing and farming with some forest industries. By mid-century, the first modest steps to industrialisation had begun with metal working and textiles. The expansion of railways from the 1860s stimulated an export trade. But without any reform of land ownership large numbers of landless peasants were condemned to a marginal existence. Between 1883 and 1917, 300,000 Finns emigrated to the US alone with tens of thousands going to Russia and elsewhere.

From the 1880s, Finland's internal autonomy came under increasing pressure from a revived Greater Russia chauvinism. Seizing on Russia's setback in its war with Japan in 1905, a broad coalition of social democrats, reform liberals, cultural and women's groups won support in the Finnish legislature for a single-chamber parliament for Finland to be elected by universal suffrage. In the 1907 election the Social Democrats, with the support of rural voters, emerged as the single largest party. In 1917 the Parliament proclaimed Finland's independence, only to be drawn into a bitter civil war between Reds and Whites (reflecting the conflict in post-revolution Russia), which claimed 15,000 Finnish lives. Despite continuing violence, the Social Democrats again emerged as the largest political party in the 1919 election and launched a programme of reform whose chief elements were a strengthening of the rights of smallholders in agriculture and forestry, the encouragement of cooperatives and the nationalisation of significant parts of the mining and wood processing industries backed by public investment.

Through a combination of agricultural protection, bilateral trading agreements and the same Keynesian policies being developed in the other Nordic countries, Finland survived the inter-war depression better than many European countries, only to fall victim again to the deteriorating international situation. Defeat in the 1939 Winter War with the Soviet Union exacted a heavy price with 25,000 dead, the loss of 12% of its national territory and the creation of 400,000 internal refugees. Finland's alliance with Germany in 1941 in an attempt to recoup its losses cost another 60,000 lives. While the Moscow Peace Agreement of 1944 restored some of the lost territories important areas containing one third of Finland's hydroelectricity output, a quarter of its chemical pulp production and 12% of its commercial forests were transferred to Soviet control and heavy reparations were imposed on its ravaged economy.

Despite these challenges, by the mid-1960s Finland had overtaken the UK in per capita wealth. Relations with the Soviet Union were stabilised by the 1948 Agreement of Friendship and Cooperation and Finnish engineering companies turned their forced dependence on Soviet markets under the reparations' obligation into an opportunity to develop a range of high technology specialist products attractive in wider markets as European and global trade were liberalised. Meanwhile Finland's global competitiveness was supported by the development of a Finnish version of Nordic 'corporatism' involving government, unions and employers in annual negotiations across the range of economic policies including legally enforceable wage negotiations (Singleton and Upton, 1998).[16]

Having built her post-war recovery on trade with the Soviet Union, Finland was again hit hard by a 60% fall in her exports to the former Soviet territory, representing 15% of total exports, following the implosion of the Soviet system from 1989. Her economic troubles were compounded by the local effects of the Nordic financial bust of the 1990s and by new competition for her forestry exports from developing countries. Between 1991 and 1993, Finland's GDP fell 10%, unemployment rose to 20% and the state was forced to take over many of the Finnish banks' toxic liabilities at a cost of around £7bn. With the added incentive of an ambition to join the euro to escape the currency fluctuations forced on the markka by dependence on a relatively narrow range of exports, Finland embarked on another round of adaptation aimed at moving the economy decisively towards a knowledge intensive and high technology base. The main vehicles were heavy investment in education at all levels, raising the combined public and private investment in Research and Development to twice the EU average at 3.5% (on a par with Sweden), and the application of a comprehensive systems approach to translating research into marketable products. By 2004, Finland had the world's highest ratio of researchers and patent applications to population in the world, had boosted high technology's share of exports to 20%, and was featuring regularly at the top of the World Economic Forum's competitiveness index. But even combined with an advanced welfare state, this record of achievement could not give Finland immunity from the global recession of the end of the first decade of the 21st century: in 2009 Finnish GDP fell by 8% before rebalancing to a projected 1.6% growth rate in 2010 with 3% predicted for 2011 and beyond.

Norway

Norway's is the best known of the Nordic histories in Scotland. Until the start of the 20th century Norway matched Finland as the poorest of the Nordic countries. Its most prominent industry was its long-distance merchant marine which, following the repeal of Britain's Navigation Laws in 1850, had expanded to become the world's third largest carrying fleet. Other economic staples were forestry and fishing along with farming, most of which, outside the south of the country, was marginal. Although poverty was not the only factor, between 1825 and 1920 nearly 750,000 Norwegians emigrated out of a population which barely exceeded two million by the beginning of the 20th century, competing with Ireland and Scotland for top place in the league of emigration loss as a proportion of population (Devine, 1999).[17]

Norway's development in the 20th century followed broadly the same path as the other Nordic countries – the emergence of a dominant social democratic party which in response to the economic pressures of the inter-war depression built a political consensus in favour of Keynesian economic policies, a corporatist system of economic governance involving government, business and the trade unions and a comprehensive welfare state.

But there are two distinctively Norwegian themes. Norway's final achievement of independence from Sweden in 1905 coincided with a public panic over fears that the source of Norway's rapidly growing hydroelectricity industry might fall under foreign control. A temporary prohibition in 1906 on the foreign purchase of waterfalls was extended in the 1917 Concession Laws to forests and mines and made applicable in principle to purchases by Norwegian companies. The motivation was as much a fear that uncontrolled industrialisation might destroy the ethos of individual and community self-reliance at the heart of Norwegian identity as a judgement of Norway's economic interest (Derry, 1973).[18] It created a presumption against allowing market forces to determine economic and social outcomes which was applied with equal enthusiasm to the development of Norway's oil reserves in the 1970s. Norway not only insisted on a slower rate of development than the UK with tighter environmental and safety laws, but made sure that the state had both a carried interest in all oil production licences and the instruments in the form of the state owned national oil company Statoil and the partly state owned Norsk Hydro (now amalgamated as StatoilHydro) to provide an alternative to the notoriously greedy multinational Seven Sisters of global oil production. The crowning piece of Norwegian oil wisdom was the creation in 1990 of a Government Pension Fund (Global) to invest a share of each year's oil revenues in an endowment for future generations. Today the Fund has a value of £300bn. Norway's combination of social democracy, selective economic nationalism and environmental activism has made her a regular contender for top place in the United Nations Development Programme's Human Development Index. In the latest Index Norway is again in top place while the UK can do no better than 28th well behind all the Nordic countries and most of the other small developed countries of Europe (UNDP, 2011).[19]

...and the Outliers

Between 1960 and 2007, the economic, though not the social record, of the Nordic countries was surpassed by Ireland. While lacking the range of natural resources enjoyed by the four core Nordic countries, Ireland successfully developed from a mainly agricultural society to a mainly manufacturing economy highly attractive to foreign direct investment, in the process moving from being a net exporter of people to a net importer. By the end of the 20th century, she had overtaken Scotland and the UK as a whole in per capita wealth, at least as measured by GDP, which includes the exported profits of multinational companies. But in a sharp reminder that small countries are not immune to policy mistakes Ireland's economic advance was put into sharp reverse by the credit crunch of 2007 which blew apart the Irish banks' grossly excessive investment in an unsustainable property boom. Having chosen in 2008 to rescue the defaulting banks from the public purse her economy suffered a 20% fall in national output and, following a bailout from the IMF and the EU of €63bn in 2010, faces several years of increasing debt to GDP ratios, rising unemployment and net emigration before she can expect to regain economic equilibrium. (Elliott, 2011).[20]

Iceland's banking crash was no less spectacular but the response by the Icelandic state was more robust. Unlike the Irish Government the Icelanders put their errant banks into administration forcing foreign bondholders to carry a substantial part of the cost rather than loading the whole burden on the shoulders of the taxpayer thereby crippling prospects for future economic recovery. By the end of 2011, the IMF was reporting that Iceland was on course for 2.5% economic growth for 2011 and 2012, against the eurozone's 1.6% and 1.1% and the UK's 0.7% for 2012 (Kerevan, 2011).[21]

Lessons for Scotland

There is a sizeable body of writing by political scientists and political economists to explain the relative success enjoyed by small developed states such as the Nordic countries, Austria and Switzerland. The cited advantages range from the benefits of the greater homogeneity of political preferences found in most small countries (Alessare and Spolare, 2003),[22] the role of short internal lines of communication and feedback creating flexibility in adapting to changes in the international environment (Katzenstein, 1985),[23] the incentives for creating niche industries (Kay, 2011)[24] and the imperative for small states to maximise the quality of their scarce human capital by high and well targeted public spending (Lindert, 2004).[25] While the banking crisis in the West and the ensuing global financial crisis have demonstrated that small states are not immune to the risks and the mistakes of larger states, their generally robust performance continues to support the thesis that they enjoy significant institutional and social advantages (Simpson, 2011).[26]

In summary, the theories postulate that shorter lines of internal communication make it easier for small countries to develop a political consensus between key social and economic interests on how to respond to new challenges and opportunities. This advantage is complemented by a high level of awareness among their populations that they must compensate for their small size by investing generously in their human resources and being flexible in responding to changes in their external environment. These attitudes have been reinforced in the Nordic countries by a relatively non-hierarchical social structure and supported historically by a homogeneous population, though in recent decades this has been eroded by an inflow of economic migrants and asylum seekers from eastern Europe and Africa.

Limits of Comparison

While these claims are plausible, they cannot be assumed to apply to all small democracies. There are important differences between Scotland and the Nordic countries. The most important is the deeper class divisions created in Scotland by a particularly rapid and harsh history of industrialisation and de-industrialisation with persisting effects in the form of significantly higher levels of poverty and inequality. Add the survival of sectarianism in parts of Scotland and London's dominance of public culture throughout the UK, and it is clear that the complementarity of structure and public culture traditionally present in the Nordic countries is absent from Scotland. On the other hand, in the last third of the 20th century Ireland demonstrated with the coordinated economic strategy promoted by Taoiseach Sean Lemass in the 1960s and elaborated by economic planning director TP Whitaker that countries, lacking the legacy advantages of the Nordic countries, could create more coordinated and effective systems of strategic decision taking than Scotland has been able to develop within the Union (Alexander, 2003; Coogan, 2004).[27]

The resilience of the small countries summarised here supports Adam Smith's consoling response to his pupil John Sinclair's lament at Britain's reverses at the hands of the North American colonies in 1781 'that there is a great deal of ruin in a nation'.[28] Of course, the record cannot provide direct evidence of how an independent Scotland would fare, except to remind us that it would be sensible to expect a mix of the good and the not so good. The logic of the Unionist argument against Scotland's independence – that independence carries no *guarantee* of economic benefit to justify the risks – is correct but irrelevant. There are, all too evidently, no guarantees of Scotland's economic success within the Union either. But expressed in terms of probability, the currency of political debate, the Unionist case gets no support from the histories of the Nordic countries or even from the records of Ireland and Iceland. Would Norway have been a more prosperous country today if it had remained under the rule of Sweden? Would Finland have done better to remain a Grand Duchy under Russian rule? Would Denmark have prospered more if it had joined Bismarck's Germany in 1864? Even taking their current economic problems into account, would Ireland have done better overall in the 20th century if it had reconciled itself to British rule or Iceland if it had integrated with Denmark? The only answer that sits comfortably with the historical evidence is: 'Very unlikely.'

Economic Particulars

The clearest economic premium from independence will come from the improved capacity to align Scottish policy with Scotland's needs and opportunities. North Sea oil provides the clearest example. It is beyond reasonable challenge that had Scotland been able to assert ownership and control of the oil reserves in the Scottish province of the North Sea in the first half of the 1970s, the Scottish economy would have derived enormous benefit in the decades since, going well beyond the boost to employment and its Barnett share of the tax revenues which it has enjoyed as part of the Union. On a conventional understanding of Scotland's national interest, independence would have led to a slower rate of oil development coordinated with a restructuring of Scottish industry, with a more demanding tax regime and a 'carried' public stake in production through a Scottish National Oil Company on the model of

Norway's Statoil combining to produce more jobs for Scotland, better protection for the environment and in many years a positive fiscal balance. In particular, the record oil revenues generated in the first half of the 1980s – £124bn (2008 prices) 1980–81 and 1985–86 – would have left a Scottish Government ample scope to meet its current funding needs and to lay the foundations for a Scottish Oil Fund (Commission on Scottish Devolution, 2009).[29]

While the peak of Scottish oil production has passed, remaining recoverable reserves in the Scottish sector are estimated at 21–35 billion barrels, between 50% and 87% of the amount extracted so far, yielding on mainstream projections of world oil prices of £5–10bn in government revenues annually over the next 40 years (Kemp, 2011).[30] Despite almost four lost decades, there is still a lot of value to be extracted from Scottish oil. Independence would also allow Scotland to benefit from the collateral value of her oil reserves and eventually of her potential in alternative energy, if that can be fully realised. Without independence, the collateral benefit accrues principally to the UK economy where much of it is dissipated by the scale of the UK's public deficit. The much larger proportionate value of the reserves to the Scottish economy would help to contain the cost of Scottish public borrowing. The Scottish budget contributed £2.6bn in 2009–10 to the cost of servicing the UK's national debt. (GERS 2009–10). The expected growth of the UK's national debt to more than 80% of GDP will increase an independent Scotland's legacy of public debt, giving increased importance to Scotland's international creditworthiness.

An independent Scotland would have had further opportunities for economising on the cost of borrowing. Under the Private Finance Initiative (PFI), imposed by the UK Treasury as the favoured source of capital investment, Scotland has committed to £6bn of PPP/PFI investment carrying a servicing charge in 2010 of £729m (GERS 2009–10) and estimated to cost the Scottish taxpayer a total of £27.7bn over the 30-year life of the contracts (Swinney, 2009).[31] Studies by the Cuthbert Consultancy suggest that the use of alternative means of borrowing could have saved the Scottish budget substantial sums. Exactly how much is difficult to establish because of the confidentiality of most PFI contracts but the Cuthberts present the cases they were able to examine as examples of a perverse principle of 'one for the cost of two' (Cuthbert, J and M, 2007).[32] More recently the UK Treasury Select Committee has suggested that PPP/PFI cost 70% more than conventional public debt (House of Commons, 2011).[33]

Another example is the Scottish fishing industry where the UK Government failed to win adequate guarantees in its negotiations for the UK's entry into the European Common Market in 1972 and in the subsequent development of a Common Fisheries Policy. Put simply, the interests of Scottish fishing did not rate highly enough in the UK's political interests to command the required negotiating clout. An independent Scottish Government giving fishing a higher priority could have put the bargaining power of her energy reserves and her right to a 200-mile exclusive economic zone behind her negotiating position. If it is assumed that an independent Scotland would have joined the EU the comparison with Norway is inexact. Nevertheless, Norway's experience provides some measure of the difference constitutional status can make. Negotiating with the EU on reciprocal fishing rights as a non-member fortified by its claim to a 200-mile exclusive economic zone, Norway's annual fish landings had declined by 2006 by 30% in volume from a 1978 peak while Scottish landings had declined by nearly 50% in 2008 from a 1985 peak (Scottish and Norwegian Governments).[34]

A third example is defence expenditure. Given the different foreign policy dynamics of a small country and the political preference of the Scottish voters, it's probable that an independent Scotland would follow a markedly different defence strategy from the UK without most of the heavy capital items considered essential by the UK to its world role such as the strategic nuclear deterrent and the Queen Elizabeth class aircraft carriers. The removal of these two items alone would save the Scottish budget around £2.2bn between 2010 and 2030, an annual average of £110m. On the same apportionment formula, on the basis of a total cost for the Iraq War to the UK of £7bn above recurring defence costs, Scotland's non-involvement would have saved the Scottish budget £600m in the years 2003–09. These sums would have been available for reinvestment in alternative jobs, including defence-related jobs, alternative energy industries or in improvements to Scotland's public services.

In support of its continuing ambition to be a world power and close ally of the US, the UK supports the world's fourth largest defence budget as a proportion of GDP. GERS 2009–10 identifies the Scottish contribution to UK defence costs as £3.1bn. If Scotland spent the same 1.5% share of GDP on defence that Norway spends on its NATO-based non-nuclear defence strategy, its annual budget would be around £2bn, allowing for a substantial conventional defence procurement budget while still releasing at least £1.1bn for non-military spending – including the creation of jobs to replace those lost by the removal of the UK's defence presence and spending programmes.

Immigration is another area where independence could benefit Scotland economically. Scotland's population is currently projected to grow by 10% by 2035, barely half the rate projected for England and marginally below the rates projected for Wales and Northern Ireland. Against a 7% increase in the working age population the population of pensionable age is expected to increase by 26% and the over-75 population by 82% pushing the dependency ratio – the proportion of the non-working age population to the working age population – from 60 (2010) to 66 per 100 (Register for Scotland, 2011).[35] But Scotland's interest in encouraging immigration has run up against the determination of recent UK Governments, facing widespread public resentment against immigrants, to pursue a conservative immigration policy which provides only limited opportunities for a different approach in Scotland.

There is a plausible case that an independent Scotland would have taken a world lead in the development of marine-based renewables. From close to the start of Scotland's oil era, the SNP was insistent that Scotland's oil wealth should be seen as a source of investment in the industries of the future, including energy conservation and alternative energy. The pioneering work undertaken by Stephen Salter in the 1970s on producing energy from waves through 'nodding ducks' won public backing from the SNP, which also voiced its strong disappointment at the closure of the UK Wave Energy Programme in 1982 following its loss of public funding reportedly under pressure from the nuclear energy industry (Harvie, 1994).[36] These are examples of big strategic decisions which independence would have allowed Scotland to take, or in some cases would still allow Scotland to take, in the Scotland's future economic interest.

Even where the benefits are difficult to quantify, their importance for Scotland's future is plain. But the role of modern government in determining the economic prospects of a country reaches well beyond these headline policies. The policies governments pursue on education and training, the environment and energy, industrial development, transport, tourism and housing, not to speak of health and economic and social equality, will be no less decisive for Scotland's future.

Economic Defects of First-Phase Devolution

Instead of challenging the inefficiencies of the way in which the UK determined economic policy for Scotland, the first phase of legislative devolution provided for in the Scotland Act 1998 simply consolidated them constitutionally. For example, the Barnett formula, which determines the size of the annual Scottish Block Grant, is applied to a series of decisions about the budgets of English spending departments without any input from the Scottish Government or Parliament. As a result decisions on the funding of English departmental budgets – for the English universities or the NHS in England – determine the Scottish budget with minimal regard to Scottish needs. Scotland's capital budget is similarly determined by Westminster needs. And at the time of writing, compared to devolved authorities in other countries Scotland's borrowing powers are severely limited. The result has been that even when confronted with exceptional opportunities for long-term development in alternative energy, the Scottish Government's capital investment is constrained within a UK straitjacket, with the added frustration that she cannot access the wealth of her current oil reserves or the potential of alternative energy as collateral.

The most damaging of the restrictions embedded in the 1998 settlement is the exclusion of any significant fiscal incentive or power for the Scottish Government to grow the Scottish economy: devolution increases its public accountability for its spending decisions but provides little incentive to grow its revenue base by boosting Scotland's economic growth and few instruments either. For example, if the Scottish Government uses part of its grant to increase expenditure on apprenticeships or training schemes for unemployed people and as a result boosts Scottish jobs, the increased tax revenues and the savings on unemployment benefits go to the UK Treasury, not the Scottish budget. The Scottish Government can look to release money by making savings in the ways it provides existing services, but the opportunities to achieve genuine savings in the short run, without undermining quality or reducing the pay of often modestly paid staff, are limited. Increased spending on early-years provision or other preventative services in the community may secure savings in the medium or longer term but in the short term they usually have to be funded by withholding other services which may be needed equally – such as youth services, more care in the community or the latest life-prolonging drugs.

The Scottish Government's 2007 proposal for a Local Income Tax which would have raised 15,000 Scots children out of poverty was in effect guillotined by the Treasury's refusal to allow the prospective savings on the UK's Council Tax Benefit (around £300m a year) to be used to support the new tax. The Treasury determined that the savings to its expenditure on Attendance Allowance in Scotland as a result of the adoption by the first Scottish Parliament of a policy of free social care should not be transferred to the Scottish budget, representing a loss of around £40m a year. Despite the Calman Commission's subsequent endorsement of the principle that such savings should be made available to the Scottish budget, there has been no change of policy by the Treasury. Even with devolution, the UK Treasury effectively has a unilateral power to interpret its own notoriously opaque spending rules. As originally conceived, the Scottish Futures Trust proposed by the SNP Government in its manifesto for the 2007 election was intended to increase the capital available for infrastructure investment through the sale of bonds direct to the Scottish public as well as to financial institutions but the proposal quickly fell to a Treasury refusal to accept the liability. Ironically, in his 2011 winter review statement the Chancellor floated a not dissimilar proposal for UK insurance companies to invest directly in his own version of an infrastructure plan for the UK.

For several years, the Treasury refused to release the £200m accumulated from the levy imposed on fossil fuel production in Scotland, even in the face of the urgent need for increased investment in the development of Scotland's green energy potential: only in late 2011 did it agree to the release of half the sum. The point is not whether a particular policy favoured by Scottish opinion would in practice benefit Scotland but that the Treasury's arbitrary power creates uncertainty for Scottish policy makers and restricts the scope and incentive for Scottish policy innovation.

Economic Challenges of Second-Phase Devolution

What if the first phase of devolution failed to equip Scotland with either the fiscal incentive to grow the Scottish economy or the fiscal and other economic policy levers to promote growth? Perhaps devolution as 'process rather than event' would be adaptable enough to repair the deficit.

The main fiscal proposal made by the Commission on Scottish Devolution (the Calman Commission) review of the first 10 years of political devolution would have obliged the Parliament to set an income tax rate for Scotland each year to replace a cut in the UK Treasury's Block Grant of the equivalent of 50% of the revenue raised in Scotland from income tax. This proposal was promoted, rather confusingly, as increasing the *accountability* of the Scottish Parliament for public spending though the text suggested that it was actually designed to promote a greater sense of *responsibility* by the Scottish Parliament and voters for public spending (Commission on Scottish Devolution, 2009).[37] Unlike the 2006 report of the Steel Commission, Calman evinced little interest in exploring changes in Scotland's fiscal powers which would give the Parliament greater power to grow the economy (Steel Commission, 2006).[38] According to two expert analyses, as translated into the Scotland Bill the proposals represent a distinct threat to the Scottish budget and risk trapping the Scottish economy in a 'deflationary threat' (Scott, 2011; Cuthbert, J and M, 2009, 2010).[39]

Either way, it was clear that the proposal by itself did little to increase Scotland's control over its economic future. It was widely criticised for leaving the proportion of Scotland's revenue base controlled by the Scottish Parliament at less than one fifth. It has even been suggested that the proposal was so problematic that it must have been designed to deter the Scottish Parliament from ever diverging from UK tax rates just as the preceding Scottish Parliaments had declined to use their power to vary the existing income tax rate by 3P in the pound (Hughes-Hallett and Scott, 2010).[40]

Calman not only failed to provide a convincing economic case but was well behind both the public debate about Scotland's economic future and the Scottish public's preference for more radical constitutional change. From 2006 there has been a flow of expert articles and reports exploring Scotland's economic options with a strong bias for greater fiscal autonomy (Steel Commission, 2006; Macdonald and Hallwood; Reform Scotland, 2008; the Scottish Government, 2009).[41]

While the return of an SNP Government in 2007 made little difference to the proportion of Scots favouring independence, it seemed to increase the proportion favouring greater economic powers for the Scottish Parliament. By 2010, 57% of Scots favoured Scottish control of taxation, 62% favoured Scottish control of welfare while 60% believed that all decisions apart from defence and foreign affairs should be made by the Scottish Parliament. Support for independence was only 23% (Scottish Centre for Social Research, 2011).[42]

Against this, the Calman Commission's proposals and the Scotland Bill which they eventually produced seemed hopelessly out of time. The explanation lay in the Commission's genesis. It was a response by the Unionist parties at Holyrood to the shock of the SNP's 2007 victory and the launch by the first SNP Government of a National Conversation on Scotland's political future. The Commission's remit was to explore any changes to the constitutional arrangements that would enable the Scottish Parliament to serve the people of Scotland better without putting at risk Scotland's devolved position within the UK.

The members of the Commission, dripping with peerages, knighthoods and other gongs from the British Government, gilded its Unionism further by pronouncing that in the interests of defending the UK's economic and social union with all its advantages for Scotland, they had been 'very careful not to make recommendations that will undermine it [devolution]' (Commission on Scottish Devolution, 2009).[43] Its aim was quickly rendered superfluous.

A year later, a Conservative-Liberal Democrat Government, with the support of barely a third of Scottish voters and a commitment to some very radical surgery on the social foundations of the Union, was in power in London; another year later a majority SNP Government with a commitment to a referendum on Scotland's independence was in power in Edinburgh. But Calman's square-wheeled barrow continued to lurch its way through the parliamentary processes of London and Edinburgh with progressively less attention given to its content and progressively more to when the barrow was going to be decommissioned.

Radical Devolution

The most radical proposals for further devolution to Scotland are promoted variously as devo plus, home rule and full fiscal autonomy (FFA), otherwise known as devo max. The first two may be seen as graduated versions of the same devolutionary coin with the fiscal and economic powers on one side and the policy powers on the other. Home rule belongs to the stuttering but persistent federalist tradition in Scotland. As a prescription for Scotland's government, it raises many of the same issues as do FFA and devo max.

The common core to all three proposals is that the bulk of the taxing, spending and other economic policy powers of government should be devolved to Scotland, leaving only the currency, defence and external affairs with the UK Government. In the version promoted by Hughes-Hallett and Scott,[44] Scotland would assume responsibility for all taxation in Scotland, including the tax base, bands and allowances, except for VAT which would be shared with the UK Government as the vehicle for Scotland's payments to the EU.

The majority of welfare payments would also be transferred, though pensions would remain a UK function, funded separately from the social security system. Through a central Grants Commission the UK and Scottish Governments would agree what payment should be made by Scotland to the UK budget in respect of the services which the UK would continue to provide and what redistribution of financial resources between UK regions might be needed. Scottish opinion would be informed and guided on the fiscal options by an independent Scottish Fiscal Policy Commission.

Full fiscal autonomy would transform the economic relationship between Scotland and the UK and for that reason has been welcomed by some Nationalists as 'independence – as near as dammit'. But how does it measure up against full independence?

The biggest shortfall would be on defence and external affairs. Under FFA/devo max, defence would remain exclusively a UK responsibility. A Scottish Parliament might, as at present, petition for the removal of nuclear weapons from Scottish territory but it could not require it. Without special provision in the legislation establishing FFA, the UK Government would be free to continue to base its nuclear missile submarines in Faslane, under its exclusive operational control, and to persist with its current programme of transferring the whole of its nuclear submarine fleet, a planned total in 2011 of 14 warships, to the Scottish base. Within such a constitutional arrangement the most that a Scottish Parliament might extract would be an explicit agreement that the UK Government accepted unlimited financial responsibility for the costs of any damage to Scotland's population, environment and economy arising from the use of Scottish territory as a nuclear base.

Based on the GERS figures, under FFA, Scotland pays each year around £3.1bn for its contribution to UK defence services and another £670m for the UK's 'external services'. (GERS 2009–10). If after the establishment of FFA, UK foreign and defence policy continued on the same lines as over the last several decades, then persuading Scottish political opinion that it was getting value for money from an annual payment of £3.7bn could be difficult. Quite apart from the persistent popular hostility in Scotland to the presence of nuclear weapons on Scottish territory, questions about the adequacy of the representation of Scottish interests in EU or wider negotiations on fisheries, climate change or perhaps environmental safeguards on deep-water oil drilling would remain as would the possibility of policy differences on issues such as UK support for US-Israeli military action against Iran or on Palestine–Israel issues. As suggested above, an independent Scotland could save around £1bn a year by adopting a Norwegian style non-nuclear defence strategy as a member of NATO or larger sums with more radical security strategies.

Another problematic area could be public borrowing within a common currency. Even with the help of the proposed central Grants Commission and independent Scottish Fiscal Policy Commission, there would be a risk of disagreement between the UK Treasury and the Scottish Government over the need and scope for public borrowing. For example, a Scottish Government might judge that Scotland's potential in alternative energy justified larger public borrowing for infrastructure investment than the UK monetary authorities were prepared to accept.

There could also be differences around competition and regulation. Under FFA, the UK would share responsibility with the EU for competition policy. But would an economically more powerful and presumably more ambitious Scotland be willing to cede responsibility for competition and financial regulation to the UK with no guarantee of direct access to EU or wider international forums? Suppose that a Scottish

Government wished to rebuild an independent Scottish-based banking sector. How would it negotiate its way through the web of UK, European and international regulation without its own representation and powers? Without the stimulus of direct responsibility and the public institutions allowing it to discharge that responsibility would it have the knowledge and confidence to conceive and design credible alternatives?

If FFA was the limit of Scotland's ambition, then its claim to the control of its geographic share of North Sea oil revenues, around 90% of the total, could well be compromised. The basis of the claim rests on the 1982 UN Convention on the Law of the Sea. As a sovereign state Scotland would have access to that and other international conventions. As a continuing part of the UK such access would be denied and her claim to the oil revenues would have to be negotiated within the UK.

Risks – Again

The Unionist case for radical devolution is that it offers the best opportunity for Scotland to enjoy a wide range of economic and other policy powers without exposing her to the risks of independence. Its appeal therefore rests on what assessment is made of the balance of risks Scotland faces – on the one hand, within the UK and on the other, as an independent country in an interdependent world. If in the Unionist lexicon of catastrophe, independence carries the ultimate risk of an economic blow-out on the scale of Ireland, continued union with the UK carries its own risks: of Scotland's best economic opportunities being sacrificed to the needs of the dominant UK economy as over North Sea oil; of the UK's politicians and regulatory authorities failing to register the dangers for the Scottish banks in the direction of development taken by the UK economy following Mrs Thatcher's Big Bang in the City in 1986; of the multiple risks, from local environmental pollution to nuclear catastrophe; or of Scotland's conscription as the UK's nuclear weapons' base. Through familiarity, the risks embedded in the status quo may seem less alarming but they are no less real than the risks of change. As Fukushima reminds us, established systems work well – until suddenly they don't.

There is a late entry to the lists of alternatives to full independence, though one which is not officially owned by any organisation. Independence-lite might be described as the unconsummated version of independence. It would go through the public rituals of a people's campaign for independence – declarations of popular sovereignty, hyped up exchanges with Unionist opponents, mass campaigns, leafleting of every household in the country – while at the same time pursuing back-channel negotiations with the UK Government to blunt the edge of some of the more intractable questions raised by independence. Candidates for negotiation would be: a defence agreement covering the continuation of UK bases in Scotland, including Faslane and continued Scottish access to UK defence contracts; an agreement on Scottish membership of sterling; perhaps shared foreign services; the common funding of pensions; and perhaps a temporary sharing of North Sea oil revenues. These would be presented – or leaked – to the Scottish public as it prepared to vote in the referendum, as understandings between two neighbouring countries for their mutual interest and therefore open to review after a respectable period. The distinction between such pre-referendum negotiations and a formal post-referendum association agreement between the two sovereign equals would be obscure and the public majority for greater powers for Scotland short of independence might be uninterested in the differences. Scotland would be formally independent but voluntarily restrained. The economic costs and benefits would be comparable to those of FFA/devo max.

Post-Crisis Options

So where did the economic case for independence stand prior to the start of the global economic crisis in 2007 on the eve of the credit crunch? In addition to the general claims about the benefits of self-determination, the economic successes of Scotland's closest international comparators provided circumstantial evidence of an independent Scotland's potential. The credibility of the core case for independence as presented by the SNP in the early 1970s had been strengthened by the revelations in 2005 and 2006 that Scottish Office and Whitehall mandarins had accepted the substance of the SNP's economic analysis. If because of the declining production and the loss of £270bn of revenues to Whitehall control in the first four decades of oil production, North Sea oil had lost some of the transformative potential acknowledged by McCrone in

1975, the remaining 21–35bn barrels of extractable oil still represented an asset of enormous value, with prices on a rising trend in anticipation of 'peak oil'.

Ten years of legislative devolution had produced two further streams of evidence – one highlighting the inefficiencies of the current limitations on Scotland's tax-raising, spending and borrowing powers, the other supporting the belief that a Scottish Government can perform with at least average levels of competence. It is not surprising that a rough consensus had developed in Scotland that an independent Scotland was not only economically viable but had good prospects of prosperity.

The Banking Crisis

In 2007 the environment was dramatically changed by the global financial crisis. By the end of 2008, Scotland's two largest banks the Royal Bank of Scotland (RBS) and Halifax Bank of Scotland (HBOS) had had to be bailed out by the UK state. There was no doubt that the collapse of the Scottish banks dealt a serious blow to Scottish pride and damaged the credibility of the SNP leadership which had cited their record as evidence that Scotland could emulate Ireland's success as a Celtic Tiger. It almost certainly contributed to the collapse of the SNP challenge to the incumbent Labour Party in the Glenrothes by-election of 6 November 2008, just two weeks after Prime Minister Gordon Brown, who held the neighbouring seat of Kirkcaldy, had carried out his emergency interventions to save the UK financial system from total collapse. It was not surprising that Labour spokespersons, led by Gordon Brown and Scottish Secretary Jim Murphy, charged that an independent Scotland would not have been able to bail out the Scottish banks.

The collapse and bailout of the Scottish banks provided the opponents of independence with some daunting figures. The liabilities of RBS and HBOS were variously estimated at between 20 and 30 times Scotland's GDP. The UK's total financial provision, including loans and asset protection for the UK banks, was £751bn of which £470bn was in respect of the two Scottish banks. While the £751bn was equivalent to half the UK's GDP Scotland's share was equal to three times Scotland's GDP (Scottish Parliament, 2009).[45] The facts appeared to leave no room for Nationalist quibbling.

But again, the first roll-call of facts was less conclusive than appeared. The charge that an independent Scotland could not have afforded to support its banks was based on several assumptions. One was that the economy of an independent Scotland would have been in the same state as the economy of Scotland as part of the UK. That was plausible only on the hypothesis that Scotland had become independent on the eve of the financial crisis with no time to repair the damaging legacy of decades of London rule. An alternative hypothesis that Scotland had become independent in, say, 1980, would give it the benefits of three decades of economic self-government, including control of Scotland's majority share of North Sea oil, in which to promote a larger and more diversified economy less exposed to the effects of the financial global crisis. This was the prospectus promoted by SNP in the 1970s and endorsed as plausible by McCrone's 1975 paper.

The Unionist argument required the further assumption that an independent Scotland would have followed the UK and Irish model of economic development with its strong emphasis on cheap credit and light regulation. This drew some plausibility from First Minster Alex Salmond's well publicised admiration for the Irish model and by hints from Finance Secretary John Swinney that he admired London's light-touch financial regulation. These attitudes referenced Scotland's options as they existed in the 2000s within the UK. It is impossible to say with certainty what policy an independent Scottish Government would have followed. It is at least plausible to suppose that, with responsibility for its own financial and economic future and equipped with the national supervisory and regulatory agencies available to the Nordic countries, it would have been more aware of the danger of allowing its indigenous banks to accumulate liabilities disproportionate to the size of its national economy.

Even on the assumption of independence on the eve of the global financial crisis, Labour's argument that an independent Scotland would effectively have been bankrupt like Iceland is grossly overstated. While HBOS and RBS had their headquarters in Scotland, HBOS's real head-quarters was in Halifax and both banks were in effect City institutions with a larger customer base, loan portfolio and staff complement in the rest of the UK than in Scotland. Out of economic self-interest, the UK Government would have had a compelling interest in collaborating with Scotland to prevent the collapse of the two banks. Even in the worst case scenario, unlike Iceland or Ireland, an independent Scotland would have had oil reserves with a wholesale worth of up to £1 trillion to mobilise as collateral for her contribution to the financial commitments required to prevent the total collapse of RBS and HBOS.

The eventual net direct financial cost to the UK taxpayer of bailing out the British banks as a whole was estimated in the 2010 Treasury Pre-Budget Report at around £10bn. The Scottish Parliament Economy Committee's report of November 2009 on the future of Scotland's financial services identifies the cost attributable to the Scottish banks at £6.5bn. On an assumption of a 50:50 shared liability, £3.25bn would have been an unwelcome addition to Scotland's financial legacy from the UK but well within the capacity of the economy to service. But within the UK the attribution of a £6.5bn cost to the Scottish account is arbitrary. The incontrovertible fact is that the Scottish banks were allowed to boom and then go bust under UK Governments and a UK policy and regulatory system, created and supervised, as it happens, by convinced Scottish Unionist politicians Gordon Brown and Alistair Darling. There are no grounds for dividing the costs of the bank bailouts by any other than the conventional UK criteria, either the Barnett formula or Scotland's share of population or GDP, between 8 or 9%.

Poisoned Legacy

Labour's citing of Scotland's banking crisis is an example of a particularly perverse category of Unionist argument against independence: the poisoned chalice argument. Such arguments highlight a structural weakness of the Scottish economy or society within the UK as a reason against independence. The near collapse of RBS is a popular exhibit. But Scotland's recent over-reliance on banking can reasonably be attributed to a historic UK policy bias in favour of the City of London, reinforced by Mrs Thatcher's Big Bang reforms of 1986 and compounded by the failure of the UK's regulatory system. It's a perverse logic which presents the Scottish consequences of these compounded UK errors as reasons for Scots to hang on to the Union rather than to discard it.

Other examples of 'perverse' argumentation against independence are not hard to find. One is the claim, revived annually on the publication of the GERS income and expenditure accounts for Scotland, that an independent Scotland would face a cripplingly large budget deficit. The fact that recent GERS accounts do not support the claim is irrelevant here. Purporting to believe that Scotland within the Union is in chronic and exceptional deficit, the opponents of independence present their factoid as a decisive argument against independence. Supporters of independence would be equally entitled to offer the persistence of such deficits as evidence that the UK is incapable of governing Scotland competently. Of course, if such large net deficits were demonstrated to exist, Nationalists would have to acknowledge that they represent a major challenge in the transition to independence but they could continue to offer it as evidence of the persistent failure of the UK's governance of Scotland. The argument that an independent Scotland could not support the burden of Scotland's health and social failures is a further example.

An optimist might hope that the disagreement could be reduced to a difference of time frame, with Nationalists agreeing that there would be a problem in the short term and Unionists conceding that in the longer term an independent Scotland would probably be able to correct the imbalance in the way that the Nordic countries were able to correct their legacy of economic and social failures in the 19th and early 20th centuries. But on neither side do the protagonists in the independence debate have much patience with timing. The effects which they claim justify their positions are all required to act if not instantaneously then within a few years and to determine the economic fortunes of the country for the foreseeable future.

Wicked Issues

There remain some individual economic arguments against independence which advocates of independence have not yet answered convincingly. Perhaps the most important relates to the currency of an independent Scotland. Since the mid-1980s, the SNP has been in favour of Scotland's membership of the EU. When the Maastricht Treaty of 1992 provided the foundations for European monetary union, the SNP adopted an 'in principle' position in favour of Scottish membership of the euro. But with the rest of the UK as its biggest single trading partner, it accepted that it would be difficult for Scotland to join the euro if

Westminster remained outside. The alternatives were to operate a separate Scottish currency aligned more or less closely with sterling or to retain sterling until either the UK decided to join the euro or the Scottish economy was judged strong enough to meet the challenge of euro membership without the rest of the UK.

For all countries except the economic superpowers, currency arrangements involve a balance of advantages and disadvantages. The range of positions among the small countries of north-west Europe illustrates the point. Ireland and Finland are members of the EU and of the eurozone. Denmark is a member of the EU and like the UK has a formal opt-out from the euro which she nevertheless uses as a peg for the Danish kroner. Sweden is a member of the EU but operates a *de facto* opt-out from the euro. Norway and Iceland are members of neither the EU nor the euro.

Each of these countries has experienced good and bad effects from their preferred currency position. Ireland enjoyed the relative stability the euro brought to its trading relationships since 1999, but at the cost of low euro interest rates which fuelled an unsustainable credit and housing boom. Finland escaped from the instability and high interest rates of its independent currency the markka by joining the euro in 2002. But in the recession of 2009, it was worrying about its loss of export competitiveness against some of its EU neighbours, including Sweden, as their currencies depreciated against the euro. By pegging the Danish kroner to the euro within a narrow fluctuation band, Denmark has enjoyed relative stability, but at the cost of having to raise its interest rates in 2008, while other countries were cutting theirs to counteract the effect of the credit crunch. The collapse of Sweden's real estate and financial boom in the early 1990s forced its central bank briefly to increase rates by no less than 500% before a tough programme of banking and budgetary reforms brought interest rate margins into close alignment with euro rates. While the Swedish currency has been relatively stable against the euro, in 2008 it fell by 20% as the Riksbank cut rates to boost the Swedish economy. Iceland, a serial devaluer of currency in the post-war era, reverted to type as part of a strategy for recovery from the 2008 collapse of its big three banks.

As a developed and diversified economy with a broad base of natural resources an independent Scotland might follow Norway and Sweden in operating an independent currency. The advantages would be a currency responsive to changes in external competitiveness and a wider margin of flexibility in monetary and budgetary policy than as part of the euro. The downside would be greater vulnerability to unwanted currency fluctuations, with generally higher interest rates to compensate.

Prior to the eurozone crisis, joining the euro while the UK retained sterling would have secured Scotland a relatively stable currency but at the risk of a loss of competitive edge in the rest of the UK, by far its largest export market. Whether membership would have served Scotland any better than it served Ireland in the run-up to the banking crisis and in its aftermath is doubtful.

There remain the options of retaining sterling or tying a separate currency closely to sterling. The SNP has proposed this last as a temporary arrangement until London decides to join the euro or failing that until Scotland is economically stable enough to join the euro on her own. The trials of the euro since the global financial crisis have made membership far less attractive to Scotland. The planned eurozone fiscal pact might well involve tighter controls over Scottish public spending than a newly independent country ambitious to compensate for years of under-investment as part of the UK could stomach.

Retaining sterling would require a political agreement with the rest of the UK. In addition to Scotland accepting UK interest rates, any agreement would limit Scotland's budgetary freedom, in respect of borrowing for example, if probably less tightly than as part of the proposed eurozone fiscal pact. And while London might agree to consult the Scottish Government on UK monetary policy, it is doubtful that it would feel any obligation to give Scotland formal representation in its monetary decisions. Pegging a separate currency to sterling would *de facto* involve some of the same constraints as sterling membership, it would invite speculative attacks at times of perceived weakness in the Scottish economy while also preserving somewhat greater freedom of fiscal and budgetary manoeuvre.

Unionists like to present the complexity of the currency choice which would face an independent Scotland as evidence that Scottish independence is peculiarly problematic. But as the experience of comparator countries shows the range of considerations facing Scotland is entirely familiar to other developed economies. Even Scotland's high level of export dependence on the rest of UK at about 70% has a parallel in Canada which sends 80% of its exports to the us. In the shadow of the world's economic superpower with a population 10 times larger than its own, Canada has seen an advantage in retaining its own currency since 1950 which despite some large fluctuations in times of economic turbulence has generally been stable against the us$. As with other countries, an independent Scotland's choice of currency arrangement will be determined by a mix of economic pragmatism and political preference.

Conclusion

The underlying foundations for the economic case for independence are the same as for the social and other cases presented here. It is not an accident that the right of the self-determination of peoples is so widely acknowledged. It reflects a judgement that those best qualified to decide how a community should manage its collective interests are the members of that community. They are in the best position to know their own needs and the best options available to them for meeting those needs. They are more likely than anyone else to be guided by an enlightened self-interest in balancing the claims of individuals and minorities within the community against the claims of the majority and of present generations against those of future generations.

In Scotland's case, most of the other things are equal. No one denies that Scotland is a nation however difficult it may be to define its identity. The right of the Scottish people to independence has been acknowledged by most of the opponents of independence within Scotland and the uk. There is no serious dispute about Scotland's boundaries, certainly none that could not be resolved by well established legal procedures. There are plenty of precedents for establishing entitlement to citizenship. Scotland satisfies all the supporting conditions for maximising the benefits of self-government – a high general level of education, a tradition of constitutional government, a developed civil society, low levels of corruption. And it has one of the world's most developed economies. What reason is there to suppose that the presumption of benefit in the maxims favouring self-determination would not apply to Scotland?

The economic evidence is diverse but strongly suggestive. There is the popular wisdom, which comes in maxims and truisms, about the social conditions and the institutional environments which support good government. There is the circumstantial evidence of the success of many of Scotland's small neighbours, qualified by the problems faced recently by Ireland and Iceland. There is the academic analysis suggesting social and institutional causes for the success of small developed states. There are above all the particulars of Scotland's circumstances, both the evident shortcomings of the current economic government of Scotland and the opportunities for alternative policies which independence would bring. And there is the balance of Scotland's economic assets and liabilities, only partially reflected in the GERS reports.

It is in the nature of political argument that an opponent of independence could present a competing set of particulars, focusing on Scotland's well known social and economic deficits and ramping up the uncertainties. But given Scotland's balance of assets and liabilities such a list simply prompts the question why has Scotland been less able over decades than most of her neighbours to mobilise the former to reduce the latter? It is hard to believe the lack of a government elected by Scots to advance their interests is not a large part of the reason.

References

1   McCrone, G, *The Economics of Nationalism Re-Examined.* Scottish Economic Planning Department, Scottish Office, 1975.

2   Kemp, A, 'The Great North Sea Oil Saga: All Done or Still Unfinished?' in Mackay, D (ed), *Scotland's Economic Future.* Reform Scotland, Edinburgh, 2011.

3   *Government Expenditure and Revenue in Scotland 2004–09,* Scottish Government, Edinburgh.

4   *Scotland: Implications for External Financing.* HM Treasury, London, 5/05/1975.

5   Darling, A, *Dialogues Concerning the Banking Crisis.* David Hume Institute, Edinburgh, 2011.

6   Darling, A, *Back from the Brink,* London, 2011.

7   *London: A Cultural Audit.* London Development Agency website, 2006.

8   Erturk, J *et al.*, *City State Against National Settlement:* UK *Economic Policy and Politics after the Financial Crisis.* Centre for Research in Socio-Cultural Change, Open University, Milton Keynes, 2011.

9   *Norway.* OECD Country Report, 2010.

10   *Report on the Way Forward for Scotland's Banking, Building Society and Financial Services Sector.* Vol. 1. Scottish Parliament Economy, Energy and Tourism Committee, Edinburgh, 2010.

11   *Platform for Success,* Scottish Government, Edinburgh, 2008.

12   *Building Economic Competitiveness: Lessons from Small Peripheral European States.* Department of Enterprise, Trade and Investment, 2011.

13   Scottish Government *Fiscal Autonomy in Scotland: The Case for Change and Options for Reform.* Edinburgh, 2009.

14   Jespersen, K, *A History of Denmark.* Basingstoke, 2009.

15   Kent, N, *A Concise History of Sweden* Cambridge University Press, 2008.

16   Singleton, F, and Upton A. A Short History of Finland, Cambridge University Press, 1998.

17   Devine, T, *The Scottish Nation 1700–2000.* London, 1999.

18   Derry, T, *A History of Modern Norway.* Oxford University Press, 1973.

19   *Human Development Index.* UNDP, 2010.

20   Elliott, L, in *The Guardian,* 28/11/2011.

21   Kerevan, G, in *The Scotsman,* 25/11/2011.

22   Alesina, A and Spolare, E, *The Size of Nations.* Cambridge, Mass, 2003.

23   Katzenstein, P, *Small States in World Markets: Industrial Policy in Europe.* Cornell University Press, 1985.

24   Kay, J, *The Economics of Small States.* David Hume Institute, Edinburgh, 2011.

25   Lindert, P, *Growing Public.* Vol. 1. *Social Spending and Economic Growth Since the 18th Century.* Cambridge University Press, 2004.

26   Simpson, D, 'An Environment for Economic Growth: Is Small Still Beautiful?' in Mackay, D (ed), *Scotland's Economic Future.* Reform Scotland, Edinburgh, 2011.

27   Alexander, W, *Chasing the Tartan Tiger: Lessons from a Celtic Cousin?* Smith Institute London 2003; Coogan, P, *Ireland in the Twentieth Century,* London, 2004.

28 Smith A, *Letter to Sir John Sinclair, 1782*, cited in Simpson, Ross I, *The Life of Adam Smith*. Oxford University Press, 1995.

29 Commission on Scottish Devolution, *Serving Scotland Better: Scotland and the United Kingdom in the 21st Century*. HMG, 2009. (See Chart 3.3: UK oil and gas taxation receipts in real terms 2008–09 prices.) HMG, London, 2009.

30 Kemp, A, 'The Great North Sea Saga' in Mackay, D (ed), *Scotland's Economic Future*. Reform Scotland, Edinburgh, 2011.

31 Swinney, J, Ministerial Answer to Kenneth Gibson MSP. Scottish Parliament, 11/02/2009.

32 Cuthbert, J and M, 'Lifting the Lid on PFI', *Scottish Left Review*, November 2007.

33 *Private Finance Initiative*. 17th Report, House of Commons Treasury Select Committee, July 2011.

34 Fisheries Statistics compiled by Scottish and Norwegian Governments.

35 *Projected Population for Scotland 2010–2035*. Register for Scotland, 2011.

36 Harvie C. *Fool's Gold: the Story of North Sea Oil*. London, 1994.

37 Commission on Scottish Devolution, 2009.

38 *Moving to Federalism: A New Settlement for Scotland*. Steel Commission, Edinburgh, 2006.

39 Scott D. *The Scotland Bill: Way Forward or Cul de Sac?* In Mackay, D (ed), *Scotland's Economic Future*. Reform Scotland, Edinburgh, 2011; Cuthbert, J and M, *Perverse Incentive of the Calman Income Tax Proposals* and *The Fiscal Trap* available on the Cuthbert Consultancy website.

40 Hughes Hallett, A and Scott, D, *Scotland: A New Fiscal Settlement*. Reform Scotland, Edinburgh, 2010.

41 The Steel Commission 2006; Macdonald, R and Hallwood P, *The Economic Case For Fiscal Autonomy*, Policy Institue nd; *Fiscal Autonomy in Scotland: The Case for Change*. The Scottish Government, Edinburgh, 2009.

42 Curtice, J and Ormiston, R, *Ready to Take Another Leap?: Public Opinion on how Scotland Should be Governed*. Scottish Social Attitudes Survey, Scottish Centre For Social Research, Edinburgh, 2011.

43 Commission on Scottish Devolution, 2009.

44 Hughes Hallett, A and Scott, D, 2010.

45 Scottish Parliament Economy, Tourism and Culture Committee, 2009.

The Social Case

Introduction

THE PURPOSE OF THIS BOOK is to assess the grounds for believing that independence would bring demonstrable benefits for Scots. We have seen that there are plausible generic, as well as particular, reasons for believing that Scotland would benefit economically from independence. The grounds for believing that an independent Scotland would be better placed to overcome her social problems are more elusive.

Scotland's Social Challenge

Scotland's social problems are well known. Scotland suffers from rates of relative poverty and ill health, of violent crime, disability and mental illness, of inequalities of life expectancy and educational attainment which are significantly higher than many of her western European counterparts. While Scotland's rate of income poverty has in the 2000s converged on and even in some years been marginally below the UK average, on most measures of social health Scotland compares poorly with the UK, which itself compares badly with most other developed countries (Maxwell, 2007).[1]

Nor is this social failure a recent phenomenon. While there are few reliable comparative figures for the inter-war decades, the available statistics suggest Scotland's social record was poor by international standards even then, consistent with the accounts of contemporaries such as the journalist George Malcolm Thomson and nutritionist and health reformer John Boyd Orr (Devine, 1999).[2]

Since the 1960s Scotland's rates of poverty and ill health have been consistently higher than those of its usual international comparators. In 2008, 21% of Scottish children were living in poverty (below 60% of median national income) compared to 9.1% of children in Denmark, 9.6% in Norway, 12% in Sweden, 12.9% in Finland and 14.9% in Austria. In the same year 17% of all Scots were living in poverty compared to 10% in Iceland, 11.3% in Norway, 11.8% in Denmark, 12.2 in Sweden and 12.4% in Austria (McKendrick *et al.*, 2011).[3]

Scotland is not alone among today's developed countries in having a history of poverty and social crisis. Ireland, Norway, Sweden, Finland and Denmark have each experienced periods of widespread social hardship and mass emigration stretching from the 19th into the first half of the 20th century. The difference is that the Nordic countries have had far greater success in overcoming their social problems: and while Ireland's recent record on income poverty is as poor as Scotland's her record in other areas is superior as reflected in longer life expectancy.

Social analysts have identified the existence of a 'Scottish effect' which produces levels of ill health in Scotland, and Glasgow in particular, above what might be expected from the currently measured socio-economic conditions. In a recent comparison of the relationship between deprivation and ill health in the UK's three most deprived cities – Glasgow, Liverpool and Manchester – with almost identical deprivation profiles, Glasgow's overall death rate was 15% higher across all ages than in the other cities and 30% higher among those under 65, with levels of suicide and addiction related deaths conspicuously higher (Walsh *et al.*, 2010).[4] Various explanations have been offered for this excess of morbidity and mortality, including unstable local populations, proximity to other areas of deprivation, and the biological effects of adverse circumstances in early life. Nor can cultural factors, whether specific to Glasgow or Scotland-wide, be ruled out. Whatever the causes, the effect adds another significant dimension to the challenges confronting Scotland's policy makers.

What explains Scotland's failure over many decades to converge on the social record of her most obvious comparator nations? It could be that the roots of Scotland's social problems are simply too deep to have allowed the rate of social improvement achieved by the Nordic countries. Great as their problems were at the beginning of the 20th century the challenge the Nordic countries faced was basically one of underdevelopment. By contrast, Scotland faced the need to sustain an advanced level of industrialisation which, for all its economic achievements, had accrued an enormous social cost in the form of appalling living conditions for a large section of the urban population. Add to that the 150,000 Scots lives lost in the First World War, exceeded as a share of population only by Serbia and Turkey among combatant nations, and the economic cataclysm of the inter-war depression compounded by the long-term attrition of Scotland's human and social capital from decades of mass emigration peaking at a massive 390,000 in the decade 1921–31 (Devine, 1999).[5] For such a battered population, the development of the British welfare state following the Second World War brought desperately needed relief.

The UK's Welfare State

The welfare state justification for Unionism begins to unravel from the 1960s as Scotland's vulnerability to the UK's long-term relative economic decline became apparent. Scottish unemployment rose above the UK trend. Emigration intensified, with graduates from the expanding Scottish universities notable contributors to the flow. Following the work of the Child Poverty Action Group and Shelter in the late 1960s in exposing the limitations of the British welfare state, in 1973 the National Children's Bureau published its *Born to Fail* report estimating that while one in 16 children in Britain were severely disadvantaged by their social and economic circumstances, in Scotland the proportion was one in ten (National Children's Bureau, 1973).[6]

Born to Fail was published as Scottish opinion was beginning to digest the prospect of Scotland becoming a major oil producer. In the Glasgow Govan by-election of 1973, the SNP's campaign contrasting the oil wealth – *It's Scotland's Oil!* – with the poverty and dilapidation evident in the constituency was considered a key factor in its unexpected victory. The Union dividend represented by the British welfare state and the package of UK regional development incentives developed in the 1960s and '70s was being outflanked by the vision of a more diversified and dynamic Scottish strategy of rebuilding its economy on the back of North Sea oil revenues.

In this alternative vision, the replacement for the failing British welfare state was a reinvigorated Scottish social democracy. The political components were at hand in the rapid decline of the Conservative vote from the 1960s, the rise of support for the SNP and to a lesser degree the

Scottish Liberals, and the durability of the Labour vote. Where Scottish politics had been principally a struggle between the Conservative and Labour parties it became increasingly a battle between the Labour Party and the SNP, both of which advertised themselves as social democratic or left-of-centre parties (Maxwell, 2009).[7]

In England the pattern was different. While both the Conservatives and Labour leaked support to third parties, the Conservatives remained Labour's principal electoral rival. The divergence between England and Scotland is revealed by the fact that of the 65 years between the end of the Second World War and the 2010 general election Scotland had a Government which it had rejected at the polls for 28 years, 18 of them between 1979 and 1997. If the Conservative–Liberal Democrat coalition constructed following the 2010 election survives for the whole of its first Parliament, the years of rejected Governments will stretch to 33 years out of 70. And since 1964, these rejected Governments have all been distinctly to the right of majority Scottish opinion as represented by Labour, SNP, and for much of the time, by the Scottish Liberals/Liberal Democrats.

The changing balance between the political parties north and south of the border was accompanied by a growing gap in the ideological balance between the two countries. This was evident less in the modest differences revealed in surveys of public opinion on left–right issues, such as the choice between improving public services or cutting taxes, the adequacy of benefit levels or the Government's responsibility to provide jobs, as in the difference in the positioning of the political parties north and south of the border. As Scottish and English voting patterns diverged, so did the respective centres of political gravity in the two countries. As the SNP increased its share of the vote in the 1970s it strengthened its identity as a social democratic party. The election of Mrs Thatcher on the back of English votes and her insistence on imposing her radical pro-market policies on Scotland, despite her rejection by 67.9% of Scottish voters, consolidated that identity. A similar dynamic, if less highly charged, operated within the Scottish Liberals (and within the short-lived Social Democrats in Scotland). While Labour in Scotland was less affected by left-wing militancy than in England, the social and economic effects of the Thatcher Governments' policies – notably the doubling in Scotland's rates of poverty and unemployment between 1979 and 1987 – reinforced the Party's faith in the public sector as Scotland's surest defence in an economically uncertain world. In a recent summary of Scotland's political values, two academics conclude that 'while simplistic views of Scotland as a naturally progressive country cannot be sustained, there is an underpinning for social democratic forms of policy' (Rosie and Bond, 2007).[8]

The existence of a social democratic bias in Scottish politics is supported by the record of the Scottish Parliament. Some of its most notable initiatives such as the introduction of free social care, the Homelessness Act, the commitment to phase out prescription charges, and the ending of the Right to Buy for new-build social housing, march easily under a social democratic banner along with the SNP Government's commitments to minimise the use of PFI/PPP, its restoration of a significant central budget to support increased house building by local authorities, its ending of a role for the private sector in Scotland's NHS, and its publication of a social policy strategy, *Achieving Our Potential*, which unusually for a Government in the UK identifies economic inequality as a cause and not simply a symptom of poverty (Scottish Government, 2009).[9]

But the restrictions on the powers of the Scottish Parliament and Government limit the extent to which the Scottish Government's performance can provide a true test of the strength of the social democratic 'underpinning' to Scottish politics. As primarily a spending authority with limited powers over taxation and no power over £16bn of welfare expenditure in Scotland or over labour market or industrial policy, how a Scottish Government would allocate public funding between social groups overall in a period of shrinking public budgets and economic depression remains largely a matter of conjecture. The most that can be said is that they would be under stronger pressure to pursue social democratic responses than governments of the UK.

Social Context

The historic reasons for Scotland's political bias to the left are less relevant here than the continuing legacy. Pro-market opponents of independence like to portray that legacy as including an unsustainable level of public spending, a swollen public sector labour force, and a high level of welfare dependency. The statistics are less emphatic. When a geographical share of North Sea oil is included in Scotland's GDP, Scotland's level of public expenditure to GDP has been lower than that of the UK since 2004–05 and close to the average for the OECD countries (Scottish Parliament Information Centre, 2010).[10] At 59%, Scotland's overall dependence on welfare payments measured by the number of Scottish households in receipt of benefits is below the UK's dependence by one point, though that average conceals higher Scottish dependence on housing benefit and incapacity and disability allowances (McKendrick, 2011).[11] Only public sector employment shows Scotland consistently above UK levels although even then the difference is modest, in 2010 23% to 20%. The marked centre-left bias of Scottish voters and the somewhat smaller bias in their policy preferences revealed in social attitude surveys may be due as much to a historic hostility to the Conservative Party as to any structural features of contemporary Scottish society.

A further reason to expect an independent Scotland to pursue a more consistent response to Scotland's social challenges lies in the social context of Scottish policy making. The UK's policy community – from think-tanks to legislators, from the civil service to the Cabinet, from the senior judiciary to senior journalists – is dominated by a middle class educated in private schools and Oxbridge. Seven per cent of the UK population at age 11 attend fee-paying schools but 35% of MPs in the new 2010 Westminster Parliament attended fee paying schools, including 15% of Labour members, and 30% of all MPs are graduates of Oxford and Cambridge, including 20% of Labour MPs (Sutton Trust, 2010).[12]

There is no information on the educational backgrounds of a wider range of Scottish elites comparable to the Sutton Trust's reports on the UK elites. However, enough is known about the educational backgrounds of MSPs to reveal the scale of their difference from MPs. Only 20% of MSPs whose educational background was known in the 2007–11 Parliament attended fee-paying schools.

The contrast between the Westminster Cabinet and the Holyrood Cabinet is even more pronounced. While 59% of the current Westminster Cabinet was privately educated and 69% attended Oxbridge, the current SNP Cabinet has no one who attended either a fee-paying school or Oxbridge while of the total of 17 Scottish Government ministers only one attended a fee-paying school and none attended Oxford or Cambridge. (Sutton Trust, 2010).[13] Indeed since the start of the Scottish Parliament in 1999 only four people educated in fee-paying schools have served in a Scottish Cabinet and only one has been an Oxbridge graduate.

This does not mean that the Scottish Parliament is socially representative of Scottish society. Only 3.3% of the members of the 2007 Scottish Parliament had a blue-collar occupation prior to becoming a parliamentarian while 73% were university or college educated (Scottish Parliament Information Centre, 2007).[14] Within the university graduates there was some bias towards universities in the elite Russell group – Glasgow, Edinburgh, St Andrews – but these universities do not have the hegemonic role in Scottish public life that Oxbridge enjoys over the public life of England and, by extension, the UK as a whole. Although there is no published research it seems likely that the family background of the majority of MSPs at Holyrood is lower-middle or working-class rather than professional or upper middle class. Surveys suggest that more Scots self-identify as working class than do English people and there is no reason to believe the same does not hold good for Scotland's politicians as well. Despite the incomplete data, it seems reasonable to conclude that the 'psychosocial' distance between Scotland's politicians and other members of Scotland's dominant public institutions and the Scottish population living on modest or poverty income, is shorter than between England's public elites and the comparable section of the English population (Wilkinson and Pickett, 2010).[15]

Scotland's social democratic bias also draws support from Scottish culture. Working-class experience features more prominently in Scottish than in English culture – for example, in the novels of Kelman and Welsh, the plays of Burke, Byrne and McGrath, the films of Mullen and Ramsay, and Scottish egalitarianism is a hardy national myth reaffirmed by the adoption of 'A Man's a Man for a' That' as the signature tune of the Scottish Parliament. In a notable example of having their cake and eating it the authors of a recent survey of poverty in Scotland report the existence of an 'abiding and potent myth in the country that people in Scotland are significantly distinctive in their ideas about poverty and welfare provision, although there is little evidence for this' before concluding that 'the political opportunities to eradicate child poverty are potentially greater in Scotland than in many other parts of the UK' (Sinclair and McKendrick, 2009).[16]

Limits to Scottish Social Democracy

Yet too much weight should not be put on these Scottish biases in favour of social democracy in assessing Scotland's social future under independence. There is little evidence that Scotland's preference for social democracy goes much beyond a belief in the protective benefits of a large public sector. The survey evidence suggesting a marginal Scottish preference for a more progressive social policy is established against the not very exacting standard of the rest of the UK, and has not been systematically assessed against a wider range of policy priorities. Nor is there any significant debate in Scotland about the policy content of a revived Scottish social democracy. Even the collapse in the global financial crisis of what remained of a Scottish-controlled banking system has so far failed to ignite a significant debate, either within or outwith Scotland's political parties, on the future economic options for Scottish social democracy. Despite the less progressive bias of English politics, the vigour and breadth of the English debate, centred in London, is far ahead of Scotland's. The fact that this in part reflects the gross imbalance in the cultural infrastructure between London and Scotland – an imbalance which Scottish independence would help to adjust – does little to counter doubts about the strength of Scotland's will for a more radical social democracy.

There is an important difference between the social case for Scotland's independence and the economic case. As we have seen, there are generic or structural as well as particular grounds for believing that independence would benefit Scotland economically. Scottish policies would be more closely aligned to Scottish preferences, needs and opportunities, while the quality of policy making would benefit from the raised levels of intelligence and imagination applied to Scottish public life. Economic growth is generally considered a public good, and public evaluation of the success or failure of economic policy depends on changes directly experienced by the majority of the public such as the availability of jobs, the level of taxes and take-home pay, and the supply of decent housing at affordable cost. While there will certainly be disputes over the allocation of scarce investment resources between competing claims or the relative priority to be given to environmental targets as against traditional economic growth, these will be disputes among minorities of the population. As the history of Gordon Brown's boasts about securing the longest period of uninterrupted economic growth between 1997 and 2007 illustrates, it is the fruits of growth or their absence, rather than the content or the sustainability of the policies responsible, which determine public perceptions.

The policies required to make inroads on Scotland's entrenched social problems cannot expect to enjoy the same degree of public latitude. The improved rate of economic growth to be expected at least in the medium and longer term under independence should make it easier to finance solutions to Scotland's social problems, but it is neither a sufficient nor a necessary condition of an effective response. The trickle-down theory of economic growth which holds that increased economic wealth would eventually percolate throughout society has been discredited by the persistence of poverty and the increase in inequality through the two decades of economic growth between the mid-1980s and the mid-2000s. The limited success of the Labour Governments of 1997–2005 in recouping the social losses suffered under the preceding Conservative regimes was due to determined efforts by the state to redistribute income from higher to lower income groups principally through the tax credits system. Children and pensioners were the chief beneficiaries in Scotland as in other parts of the UK with a 25% drop in child poverty rates in Scotland by 2005. But by 2006, progress had stalled and, with the onset of the recession, was threatening to go into reverse. In 2008–09, nearly one in five Scots continued to live in relative poverty including just over one in five Scottish children (McKendrick, 2011).[17]

The measures required to reduce Scotland's poverty to levels similar to the Nordic countries, approximately half the Scottish level, will need to go well beyond the selective social democratic programmes implemented by the UK Labour Governments between 1997 and 2010 or the slightly more ambitious plans sketched by the SNP Government of 2007–11 (Scottish Government, 2009).[18] Currently there is a wide gulf between Scotland's default social democracy and the policies needed to make serious inroads on Scotland's social problems. The missing policy package would need to include a further substantial redistribution of income from the top two or three income deciles to the bottom two or three through the tax and benefit system: higher taxes on capital wealth; increased support to improve the health and education of the most disadvantaged communities and households; new ways of ensuring that children from the poorest homes access the full range of further and higher education; a large increase in early years' prevention and the introduction of a Living Wage to combat 'in work' poverty.

Inequalities of political power will also need to be reduced by further reforms to national and local government, for example, the extension of STV to national elections and provision for national and local initiative referenda, and by the direct empowerment of local communities. People will need to be given more opportunities to gain control over their personal and collective public services through the extension of individual budgets and local mixed markets of service provision democratically managed at local level to maximise community benefit. The public interest in a more stable and predictable economy will have to be asserted, both through selective interventions by the central state to compensate for the weaknesses of Scotland's banking system following the crisis, and through the promotion of the social economy in the shape of community ownership, mutuality and stakeholder representation. Even reform on this scale would carry no guarantee of bringing Scotland's rates of poverty down to Nordic levels.

Problematic Politics

The politics of reform on a Nordic scale would be distinctly problematic. Scottish public opinion may be sympathetic to further reform of Scotland's government as part of the devolution process but the more egalitarian tax and spending policies characteristic of the Nordic societies would encounter stiff opposition from powerful middle-class and business interests. There is nothing in Scotland's recent political record to suggest a pent-up demand for radical social and economic change waiting to be released by independence. Mainstream Nationalism as represented by the SNP is predicated on attracting support from a significant portion of Scotland's business community: in a political culture as cautious and defensive as Scotland's, such support may be a necessary condition for achieving independence but it is also a potential obstacle to radical reform following independence. Meanwhile, as we have seen, many of the social and cultural forces which have shaped the welfare nationalism of the Nordic countries are absent from Scotland.

Under these limiting circumstances progress on social reform would depend on two factors – the scope for increasing the effectiveness of social policy under independence within the existing balance of political forces, and the potential for constructing a wider progressive alliance led by civil society as a counterweight to the influence of the business community and some sections of the middle class.

Evidence submitted to the Commission on Scottish Devolution by civil society organisations, including voluntary organisations on the front line of action against Scotland's social problems, reveals a belief that significant scope exists for improving the effectiveness of Scottish social policy. Submissions include calls for the transfer to Scotland of the main responsibility for the tax and benefit system (the Church of Scotland); of Housing Benefit and Council Tax Benefit (Royal Society of Edinburgh, the STUC); of Housing Benefit as part of a package embracing other tax, welfare, labour market powers and energy regulation (Scottish Federation of Housing Associations); of skills training and labour market powers (Scottish Council for Voluntary Organisations); of equalities legislation, specifically equalities for disabled people (ECAS, SCVO); and of the funding of childcare programmes (Children in Scotland). In most cases the recommendations are justified as reducing confusion and creating opportunities for better coordinated responses without any detailed policy recommendations. In other words they depend on familiar maxims about the benefits of decentralised decision taking: the Church of Scotland prefaces its evidence with a statement of the subsidiarity principle – 'that nothing shall be done by a larger and more complex organisation which can be done as well by a smaller and simpler organisation' (website of the Commission on Scottish Devolution, 2009).[19]

What of the prospects for a progressive alliance to extend the constituency for a more radical reform programme? Many of the key groups in Scottish civil society – the voluntary sector, the churches, the trade unions, the mutuals, the environmental campaigners – already have organisational and personal links, and in a small country the task of extending the network to other groups and movements is manageable. Many of the groups also advocate radical change within their own fields of interest. The central challenge is to fuse these disparate claims in a programme of sufficient credibility to exert significant leverage on political parties and on government. Where is the shared ground between green activists, trade unionists, human rights and equalities campaigners, social care voluntary groups, land reformers, nuclear disarmers, anti-poverty activists, campaigners for community empowerment, advocates of mutuality and other important players in Scottish civil society? And if a platform could be agreed how would it be made relevant to the more immediate concerns of the public and thus of the political parties? Jobs and the economy would have to be at the heart of any common platform with ambitions to influence the political parties and a future Government. Scotland's potential for developing a low carbon economy is one obvious element though it would have to be more clearly linked to community ownership and the prevention of fuel-poverty. Reconstructing Scotland's banking system on a model which provides a stable source of credit for Scottish families and businesses and of longer-term investment capital is another. The ultimate challenge would be integrating a credible economic and environmental programme with the needed social and political reforms. In Scotland's conservative political culture, neither the vision nor the reality of independence can be counted on to generate such radicalism. There are alternative models on offer of Scottish society under independence and other less radical strategies for achieving them.

What could reasonably be expected from independence is a sharpening of the sense of Scottish responsibility for Scotland's social health. At the least it would rob Scots of their alibis for failure, increasing the pressure on them to confront the areas in which as a society they fall short of the performance of the best in Europe. And it should make them more receptive to one of the key lessons of the Nordic experience, that a small country has to make its living from its own assets of which the most critical is its own people.

Economic Realities

The challenge of doing that as an independent country supporting an advanced welfare state in the aftermath of the worst economic crisis in the post-war period is formidable. Since the beginning of the 2007–08 economic crisis Scottish political opinion has been treated to a crash course of education in the new economic realities with much of the material provided by reports commissioned by the SNP Government.

Three major challenges have been highlighted. One is the recurring cost of Scotland's past social failures. Even in the absence of the UK's fiscal crisis, the cost of 'failure demand' – that is, the demand for public services created by preventable failures in individual and community lives – would put future Scottish budgets under severe strain. The Improvement Service suggests that dealing with failure demand absorbs around 40% of Scottish local authorities' service budgets. During the early devolution years when the Westminster grant was increasing annually in real terms by 3–4% it was possible to absorb that but over the next 15 years – when according to the Independent Budget Report Scotland stands to lose £39bn from her spending – that will be impossible, not least because the cutbacks in service spending will be steadily adding to the future level of failure demand. (Mair *et al.*, 2011).[20]

The second major challenge is the cost of the ageing of Scotland's population and the projected increase in Scotland's dependency ratio. The Christie Commission on the Future Delivery of Public Services estimates that over the next 15 years the cost of the additional demand in health, social care and justice alone will amount to £27bn (Commission on the Future Delivery of Public Services, 2011).[21]

The third challenge is the increased cost of servicing Scotland's inherited share of the UK's national debt officially projected to rise from its current 62% of GDP (2011) to 71% in 2013–14, but expected by many analysts to rise to well beyond 80% (Office of Budget Responsibility 2011).[22] The Office expects the UK Government's annual debt interest payments to rise from £48bn in 2010–11 to £66bn in 2015–16. On the assumption that an independent Scotland could sell debt on the same terms as the UK, that would leave an independent Scotland with an inherited annual debt payment bill from 2015–16 of double the £2.6bn Scottish contribution to servicing the UK national debt estimated by GERS for 2009–10.

Advocates of independence can argue that with freedom to set its own budget and with control of its oil revenues an independent Scotland would be fiscally more robust than the UK. That could well be the case though as a major oil producer Scotland's fiscal prospects as an independent state or a fiscally autonomous territory within the UK would be fully exposed to the unpredictability of oil prices without the fallback stabiliser of the UK's much bigger tax base.

Political Challenge

The political challenge is equally daunting. Much of the failure demand Scotland faces has its roots in the deep inequalities in Scottish society. Confirming what other more specialised studies of inequality in Scotland have shown the Improvement Service notes that 'where Scotland is starkly different from other European countries is... in the extreme variation around the average' (Mair *et al.*, 2011).[23] It cites the case of Scottish education which, despite an average performance putting it fifth in Europe ahead of Norway, Sweden, England and France, reveals a bigger gap between the qualifications of the top 20% and the bottom 20% of school students than anywhere else in Europe. One reason is the high clustering of mutually reinforcing problems in the most deprived neighbourhoods. Many of these will be among the worst deprived 15% of Scottish communities which, with less than one seventh of Scotland's population, are home to one third of its 'income deprived' population (Scottish Government, 2010).[24] Over the last four decades hundreds of £millions of public money have been spent trying to reduce the deprivation in such area based concentrations with only limited success. Effective action will require not only big changes in the ways central and local government deliver public services, including the direct empowerment of service users and communities, but also a sustained assault on the overall levels of inequalities of income and wealth in Scotland.

Conclusion

The social case for independence rests on five grounds: the maxim that those who best know a problem are best equipped to solve it; a reasonable expectation that independence will strengthen Scotland's economy and public revenues; Scotland's record of consistent support for social democracy, the only ideology of current political relevance offering a foundation for combating inequality in a mature welfare state; a reasonable expectation that the quality of Scottish policy making will improve as government and civil society respond to the stimuli of increased responsibility; and a reasonable belief that the integrated policies required for effective action against complex social problems are more likely to be provided within a single political authority than by divided authorities. These are grounds to anticipate progress but they fall well short of providing a route map to Nordic levels of equality and welfare.

References

1   Maxwell S, 'A Poor Response' in Brown, R (ed), *Nation In a State*. Dunfermline, 2007.

2   Devine, T, *The Scottish Nation 1700–2000*. London, 1999.

3   McKendrick, J *et al.*, 'Is Poverty Falling?' in McKendrick J *et al.* (eds), *Poverty in Scotland 2011*, CPAG London, 2011.

4   Walsh, D *et al.*, *Investigating a 'Glasgow' Effect*. Glasgow Centre for Population Health, 2011.

5   Devine, T, *The Scottish Nation 1700–2000*. London, 1999.

6   *Born to Fail*. National Children's Bureau, London, 1973.

7   Maxwell, S, 'Social Justice and the SNP' in Hassan, G (ed), *The Modern SNP: From Protest to Power*. Edinburgh, 2009.

8   Rosie, M, and Bond, R, 'Social Democratic Scotland?' in Keating, M (ed), *Scottish Social Democracy: Progressive Ideas for Public Policy*. Brussels, 2007.

9   *Achieving Our Potential*. Scottish Government, Edinburgh, 2009.

10 *The Size of the Public Sector*. Scottish Scottish Parliament Information Centre, 2010.

11 McKendrick, J, 'What is Life like for People Experiencing Poverty?' in McKendrick J *et al.* (eds), *Poverty in Scotland 2011*, CPAG London, 2011.

12 The Sutton Trust *The Educational Background of Members of Parliament*, May 2011.

13 *The Educational Background of Government Ministers*. The Sutton Trust, July 2010.

14 *Election 2007*. Scottish Scottish Parliament Information Centre, 2007.

15 Wilkinson, R and Pickett, K, *The Spirit Level*. London, 2010.

16 Sinclair, S and McKendrick, J, *Child Poverty in Scotland: Taking the Next Steps*. Joseph Rowntree Foundation, 2009.

17 McKendrick, J *et al.*, 'Is Poverty Falling?' in McKendrick J *et al.* (eds), *Poverty*

in Scotland 2011, CPAG London, 2011.

18 *Achieving Our Potential.* Scottish Government, Edinburgh, 2009.

19 Commission on Scottish Devolution website, 2011.

20 Mair, C *et al., Making Better Places: Making Places Better.* Scottish Government Improvement Service Edinburgh, 2011; *Independent Budget Report.* Scottish Government, Edinburgh, 2011.

21 *The Commission on the Future Delivery of Public Services.* Scottish Government, Edinburgh, 2011.

22 *Economic and Fiscal Outlook, March 2011.* Office of Budget Responsibility, HM Treasury, 2011.

23 Mair, C *et al., Making Better Places: Making Places Better.* Scottish Government Improvement Service Edinburgh, 2011; *Independent Budget Report.* Scottish Government, Edinburgh, 2011.

24 *Scottish Index of Multiple Deprivation: Update, 2010.* Scottish Government, Edinburgh, 2011.

The International Case

Introduction

THERE ARE TWO TESTS to apply – would independence increase Scotland's ability to defend her national interests in international affairs, and would Scotland's independence be more likely to increase than diminish prospects for world development?

It is possible, of course, that the interests of a small country may coincide so closely with those of a larger neighbour as to make independence appear unnecessary for foreign policy purposes: or, if a smaller country's interests diverge from those of a larger neighbour its international environment may make independence appear too risky, or perilous. Neither possibility matches Scotland's circumstances. The political differences summarised below preclude the first possibility and are reinforced by divergent social, economic and cultural needs and preferences. For most Scots, the second possibility – that independence is desirable but too risky – probably carries more resonance. Below, I argue that while the international environment would present challenges for an independent Scotland overall, it would be strongly supportive of Scotland's independence.

The Possibility of Independence

Before examining the international case for Scotland's independence, a prior question that is frequently posed has to be answered. Is independence possible in an increasingly interdependent world? There is a widespread view that interdependence has made independence impossible for all but the very largest states, often countered by Nationalists with the claim that the independent states in membership of the UN have grown from 51 in 1945 to 192 today, of which about half have a smaller population than Scotland.

It comes down to what is meant by independence. If it is understood as self-sufficiency then no modern state is independent. With the growth of interdependence in the years since the Second World War, every state is located somewhere on a broad spectrum of capacity for effective unilateral action, with the US at one end with a battery of feasible options in most circumstances, and a South Pacific micro-state at the other with little option but to appeal to international opinion. At what point on the spectrum a state meeting the criteria for membership of the UN is revealed as not really independent provides scope for endless debate. How little independence is no independence at all?

The institutional response to the growth of interdependence has been the development of formal agreements between states to pool their decision making, of which the UN and its agencies, collective security agreements like NATO, the EU and the EEA are three very different examples. The prolific growth of such agreements in the post-war period has persuaded many academic analysts that the concept of the state as the possessor of a presumptive sovereign authority is redundant along with forms of political nationalism focused on the achievement of state independence.

In this 'post-sovereign' world, the best option for communities seeking greater powers of self-determination is to find a constitutional status which allows for the maximum mobilisation of the community's internal resources in support of its development, while managing its international interdependence by pooling its sovereign powers with other states with shared interests and values. For Scotland, the only feasible option is presented as Scottish autonomy short of independence within some reconfiguration of the Union within an integrating Europe. In almost all versions of the post-sovereignty thesis the maximum autonomy available to Scotland stops short of Scotland having authority over her foreign policy and defence and in most versions over currency (Paterson, 1994; MacCormick, 1999; Keating, 2009).[1] It follows that there can be no case on international grounds for Scotland's independence.

There are several problems with these attempts to assign Scotland a future as a 'nation' region of the EU. First, they overstate the impact of the growth of interdependence on states' unilateral power of action: for example, in the Scottish case they fail to acknowledge that an independent Scotland would have the same sovereign rights to her marine and seabed resources as other independent countries such as Norway, along with the benefits those rights would bring. Second, they ignore the importance to Scotland of asserting a sovereign right to determine her own defence posture in the light of the security and economic costs of her assigned role in the UK's nuclear defence strategy. Third, their analysis – at least until the eurozone crisis – sat uncomfortably with the range of relationships actually available to members of the EU in its notably pragmatic course of development since its foundation in 1957. Fourth, their accounts underestimate the tension between popular sovereignty and the anti-democratic tendencies of the Union's centralising political dynamic as illustrated most recently in its response to the eurozone crisis.

National Security

National security is conventionally seen as the greatest problem facing small states. When the claim for Scotland's independence was a focus of political argument in the 1970s, the security risks to which independence might expose Scotland were a major debating point. Scotland was located in a militarily sensitive region of the Cold War only 200 miles east of sensitive Nordic frontiers with the Soviet Union and on the western flank of the Greenland-Iceland-Faroes gap critical for the Soviet Navy's access to the Atlantic. The discovery in the middle of the Cold War of major oil reserves in the Scottish province of the North Sea added to the sense of vulnerability.

Even in the Cold War, these fears were exaggerated. As the West's collective response to the Soviet threat, NATO provided a supportive security framework for the small democracies of western Europe while allowing them significant latitude on their role including the stationing of nuclear weapons on their national territories. It was not difficult for the SNP to offer a plausible security strategy for Scotland as a non-nuclear member of NATO on the Norwegian model (Maxwell, 1977).[2]

Following the end of the Cold War an independent Scotland would be free of any significant security threat from within her regional environment. Indeed the overall environment for small states in western Europe is in historical terms unusually benign. The greatest threat to Scotland's security comes not from any external source but from the risks associated with its assigned role in the UK's nuclear defence strategy.

The international case for Scotland's independence should be assessed against two main criteria – whether independence would increase Scotland's ability to promote her legitimate national interests, and whether it would be more likely to increase than diminish prospects for world development. It is also worth asking – how might Scotland's engagement with international affairs as an independent state affect Scotland's public culture?

Unionist Assumptions

Many Unionists find it difficult to take such questions seriously. To them, the international advantages of Scotland being part of a Union which is the world's fourth largest defence spender, a member of the world's nuclear club, a member of the G8 and G20, and a permanent member of the UN Security Council, are self-evident.

The Commission on Scottish Devolution was, of course, precluded by its remit from considering any constitutional option for Scotland incompatible with the Union. It nevertheless felt compelled to advertise its faith in the necessity of the Union in international affairs: 'in a world with rapidly changing and uncertain threats, all parts of the UK must remain joined together for defence and national security... we are clear that it is in Scotland's interests for the UK to discharge the international functions and obligations of the sovereign State towards other states'. Faith needs no justification and received none (Commission on Scottish Devolution, 2009).[3]

The report of the Steel Commission – *Moving to Federalism: A New Settlement for Scotland* – largely shared the faith. The indispensability of the Union is simplistically asserted. Whatever measure of political decentralisation may be desirable in the name of federalism, it should stop well short of putting at risk the self-evident benefits of the Union's world role. 'The UK Government is best placed to deal with issues that affect the whole island – foreign affairs, defence, immigration policy, macro-economic policy, macro-economic affairs, trade laws.' Even where it gives a nod to the need for justification it simply reveals the circularity of its Unionist reasoning: 'The Union enabled Scotland to punch above its weight on the world stage and allowed Britain to become more than its parts... the UK as a whole has a greater punch internationally than any of its constituent parts separately... This [the Union] enables us to have more influence in Europe, the United Nations, NATO and other international bodies than we would otherwise have' (Steel Commission, 2006).[4]

This avoids the obvious questions – who are the 'we' and has that 'greater punch' generally been deployed to promote Scottish interests and policy preferences? The truth is that the most obvious external advantages of the Union to Scotland derived from the empire, which brought major economic benefits, though at a high price in lives lost in imperial wars. While the longer-term economic legacy of empire has been ambivalent for the UK as a whole, Scotland's portion – lacking the benefits which accrued to England as the home of the former imperial capital and of the empire's dominant elites while leaving Scotland's economy trapped in a dependent provincial role – has been particularly problematic.

The international benefits to Scotland of the Union after empire are more elusive. Imperial preference is long gone. Scotland's current interests as a trading nation are now supported by a web of regional and global trade agreements to which the UK is one signatory among many of differing sizes of population and economy. As an independent country Scotland would have the same access to regional and world trade agreements and markets as are available to other members of the international community, topped up where necessary by bilateral agreements.

The bulk of trade negotiations are now carried on in multilateral forums and are often subject to judicial process, as with the Scotch Whisky Association's successful case in 2007 to the World Trade Organisation (WTO) against excessive duties imposed by the Indian Government on Scotch whisky imports. Where the process is political rather than judicial, as in the WTO's prolonged Doha round of world trade negotiations or in EU trade talks, it is debatable whether Scotland gains more in negotiating clout from being a part of the world's seventh largest economy than she loses from having only modest influence over the ranking of Scottish interests in the UK's negotiating platform. The UK's record in defending Scotland's fishing interests in the EU suggests that the negotiating benefits of Union membership are exaggerated. The record of the smaller developed countries, whether or not they are members of a collective negotiating body such as the EU, does not throw up any conspicuous victims of long-term trade discrimination – with the possible exception of New Zealand – following the UK's entry to the Common Market in 1973. As the example of Norway suggests, a small country able to concentrate its legal claims, bargaining resources and negotiating skills behind a vital commercial interest is at least as likely to succeed than a territory whose interests are subordinated to the negotiating priorities of a central government.

Those prospects are influenced by the small country's degree of dependence on a dominant partner. That is why in the post-war period the Benelux and Nordic countries and Ireland, for example, have been keen to dilute their dependence on their dominant neighbours by multilateral trade agreements or economic unions. In her trading relationship with the rUK, an independent Scotland would benefit from the guarantees of open markets under both EU and global trading agreements. In addition, Scotland could expect to negotiate further assurances bilaterally with the rUK for whom she would continue to be both an important export market and provider of energy.

EU *Transition*

There is an argument that Scotland would be denied a seamless transition into full membership of the EU as a successor state or even that it might be denied membership altogether. (Murkens *et al.*, 2002; House of Commons, 2011).[5]

Much would depend on whether Scotland would be treated as a successor state to the UK – and so inherit the EU rights and obligations accumulated by the UK – or as an entirely new state with no pre-existing rights and obligations. In the absence of any precedent for part of the territory of a EU member state becoming independent and wishing to remain part of the EU, there is no clear answer. But whatever the technical legal arguments around Scotland's succession rights, it is unlikely that they would be allowed to outweigh the EU's political interest and established practice.

The EU has adopted eligibility criteria for EU membership (Article 2 of the Treaty of Union and the 1993 Copenhagen criteria) – including a stable democracy, a commitment to human rights and the rule of law, open markets, a sound fiscal position, and a commitment to adopt existing EU policies – which Scotland, with one possible exception, would have little difficulty in meeting. In its own interests, the EU would hesitate to alienate a country which was an important energy producer and possessed substantial fishing reserves of interest to several of its member states.

The prospect that some EU states, notably Spain, would resist Scotland's membership on the grounds that it might encourage their internal independence movements has been a particular focus of speculation. Spain and Belgium face significant challenges from independence movements in Catalonia and Flanders respectively. But as argued throughout this book, the logic of independence is particular. Both the Flemish and Catalan challenges are responses to their particular circumstances. The Flemish are unlikely to be influenced by Scotland's entry to the EU as an independent state: they follow their own dynamic. The evolution of their political ambitions in the heart of Europe is likely to have a greater impact on the future shape of the EU than the membership of an acknowledged historic nation and geographical outlier such as Scotland.

Catalan support for independence is increasing, following a decision of the Spanish Constitutional Court in 2010 to strike out key provisions in a statute jointly ratified by the Spanish and Catalan parliaments giving Catalonia important new powers. Some recent polls (2011) show support for independence as high as 40%, though most commentators believe that if an official vote were held independence would struggle to achieve half that. The outcome of any significant independence campaigns by the Catalans – or the Basques – would be likely to depend much more on the internal politics of Spain, particularly the constitutional entrenchment of Spain as a unitary entity, than on the fate of a Scottish application for membership. Manuel García-Margallo, the Spanish Minister for Foreign Affairs and Cooperation, has stated that in the event of Scottish independence, 'Spain would have nothing to say. We would simply maintain that it does not affect us' (García-Margallo, 2012).[6] In any event there would be limits to the indulgence Spain would be given by its fellow EU members to dictate EU policy in pursuit of its own constitutional interest, especially in its weakened economic position. The EU would have to have some regard to consistency with its own eligibility criteria and its past flexibility in accepting applications from new members within the last 10 years some of which were far less able to satisfy the established criteria for membership than Scotland, as well as to the treatment of the current application by Iceland and the possibility of future applications by Norway and Switzerland.

Acquis Communautaire

One complication in Scotland's approach to Europe would be Scotland's attitude to the *acquis communautaire,* the accumulated legacy of EU policy which new member states are expected to adopt. That legacy notoriously includes a fishing policy which Scotland opposes but of which Spain is a major beneficiary. A Scottish insistence on making reform of the common fisheries policy a key negotiating demand could give Spain a more respectable pretext for vetoing Scotland's membership than any concern for internal political consequences. Scotland would have to decide what priority to give to its fisheries interests in the entry negotiations as opposed to reserving her right to make the case for reform as a future member within the more restrictive processes of the EU's decision taking. The strong probability is that whatever the lawyers' views on succession rights, the EU's decision on Scotland will be a political one in which a combination of the benefits Scotland would bring to it and the embarrassment which the EU would suffer by a rejection of one of Europe's historic nations and established democracies would work in Scotland's favour.

The *acquis* also includes an obligation on new members to join the euro after a transitional period. As a successor state to the UK, Scotland would enjoy the benefit of the formal opt-out negotiated by the UK at Maastricht in 1992. Even without successor state status, Scotland should be able to benefit from the EU's record of flexibility. Sweden without a formal opt-out has remained outside the euro and looks unlikely to join any time soon and only five of the 12 new members which joined the EU in 2004 have so far joined the euro. It would be difficult for the EU to apply a more rigorous rule on the euro to Scotland than to Sweden or the other non-joiners. If Scotland were to insist, as several members of the EU have done, that any decision on the euro must be subject to a popular vote it would be even more awkward for the EU to insist on membership regardless.

Depending on the development of Scottish politics up to the point of independence, other elements of the *acquis* could prove problematic for Scotland. The *acquis* embraces the single internal market (1992) and the Maastricht Treaty (1992) which would impose significant restrictions, in principle if less consistently in practice, on a range of state powers. For example, the limitation on the powers of national governments to control the movement of capital makes it more difficult to defend national ownership of economies or national business champions from takeover by external capital. Scottish policy would be subject to Brussels' competition rules as UK policy is. To take a topical issue, if Scotland wanted to rebuild an independent banking sector from the ruins of the 2008 crisis the EU's freedom for capital movements and rules against distortions of markets arising from preferential tax treatment or other forms of public subsidy would significantly limit the options.

Membership of the EU, let alone of the eurozone, is not a necessary condition of Scotland's independence. If the EU were to make its conditions for Scottish membership too rigorous Scotland could opt to remain outside as a member of the European Economic Area (EEA) or in a bilateral relationship like Switzerland. Neither of these would offer Scotland a free ride. As a member of the EEA enjoying access to EU markets, Scotland would have to accept many of the rules of the single market and contribute to the costs of the EU institutions and some of its programmes. But she would enjoy greater freedom of action than as a EU member, certainly than as a member of a tighter eurozone. She could reclaim control of her fisheries, collaborate with Norway and other territories of the north-west Atlantic to protect the management of their marine resources from EU interference, and avoid European centralisation of control over their finances.

The Wider World

Succession rights would be a less significant issue for Scotland's participation in wider structures of global government. International recognition as an independent state would qualify Scotland for direct representation in the UN and its agencies such as the World Trade Organisation and the UN Convention on the Law of the Sea, international fishing conventions, the International Telecommunications Union, the UN Framework Committee on Climate Change, collective security organisations such as NATO and the Organisation for Security and Cooperation in Europe (OSCE), the Nuclear Non-Proliferation Treaty (established in 1974 at the instigation of two small countries Ireland and Finland), the International Energy Agency, the International Atomic Energy Authority (IAEA) and many others. As the record of Ireland, Finland, Sweden and Norway demonstrates, small states can play constructive and sometimes path-breaking roles in international affairs.

Scotland's participation in global affairs as an independent state could bring important internal benefits. The least plausible of the Unionist arguments against independence has been the charge that the dissolution of the Union would turn Scotland into a political kailyard. When most Scots viewed the world through the prism of empire, separation from the imperial heartland might have produced severe withdrawal symptoms. But in an age of global interdependence and instant communication, London's monopoly of official representation and its dominance of media and cultural representations of the world to the UK and of the UK to the world, appear to many Scots to impose their own form of separation. 'Stop the World – we want to get on' was Winnie Ewing's cry in 1967 and its relevance and urgency has increased with the growth of global interdependence in the intervening decades. Isolation and separatism are simply not options for a developed economy and society in the early 21st century. Even if Scotland's own history before and and after the Union had not planted a strong sense of international connectedness in the Scottish imagination, her self-interest as a society and culture requires that she educates herself in the complexities and opportunities of the contemporary world.

It would be wrong to charge Unionists with being the parochial ones now, but the symptoms of delusion and sentimentality about Great Britain's significance to the world are easy to see in the British political elite's obssession with maintaining the UK as a world nuclear power with a wide-ranging spectrum of military capability whatever the strain on already constrained public budgets.

Today, Unionists are more likely to complain of the financial cost to Scotland of independent participation in global governance than of the danger of a regression to the kailyard. The costs would be significant but Scotland already contributes to the cost of the UK's external representation – to the tune of £670m, according to GERS 2009–10 – and other small, developed countries manage to fund their participation in global affairs. There would be every prospect of offsetting economic benefits, not just in the promotion of Scotland as an economic partner and as an international 'brand', but also through increased awareness among Scots of the opportunities and risks of their international environment. So the cost of Scotland's participation in global governance should be seen not just as a way of ensuring that Scotland's interests are represented in international forums but as an investment in Scotland's institutional and intellectual capital generating a range of benefits, including a more sophisticated public understanding of her international environment and a more diversified and export-oriented economy.

If the international economic environment is reasonably sympathetic to small, independent, developed economies, the security environment for small European states is emphatically so. With the end of the Cold War there is no security threat to Scotland from within the European theatre. The issues between the Russian Federation and Norway over the future control of the High North – the Barents Sea and the eastern Arctic Ocean and their resources – were settled in spring 2010 with agreement for the roughly equal division of control over 175,000 square kilometres of marine territory and for cooperation on fisheries and oil exploration. If proof was needed that in an interdependent 'rules-bound' world, small countries can secure their rights – even in the face of a gross disparity of size and military power – then this case provides it.

As the Arctic ice cover retreats, the extended High North from the Bering Strait to the Denmark Strait will attract increased international competition for its marine and sea bed resources. Over the last several years, in response to the uncertainties in the High North, Norway has increased her defence expenditure above the Nordic average and even after the recent agreement with the Russian Federation is likely to maintain the increased level. While Scotland will certainly have an interest in developments in the High North she will remain a second line player behind Canada, the US, Russia, Norway and Denmark (on behalf of Greenland and the Faroes), leaving her with scope to reduce her defence expenditure below its current ratio to GDP as part of the UK to something closer to the Nordic average of 1.5%, or lower, if she opts for more radical security strategies.

The current wisdom is that the most serious security threat to the UK is the threat of terrorist attack. Scotland, of course, has been the scene of one such attack, at Glasgow Airport in June 2007. The scale of the threat is impossible to estimate with the publicly available information, but it is reasonable to expect that it would be reduced rather than increased by Scotland becoming independent. The UK's imperial past, including its contemporary status as staunchest ally of the US in the war on terrorism, identifies it as an obvious target for extremists. While the political symbolism of an episode of constitutional change in a corner of north-west Europe is not likely to be of overwhelming interest to the leaders of al-Qaeda in the Yemen or Somalia they might eventually pick up an international reading of Scotland's parting from the UK as a Scottish judgement on UK foreign policy. Meanwhile the foreign policy positions adopted by Scotland on such litmus paper issues as Palestine, Iran's nuclear ambitions or participation in Western interventions such as Iraq or Afghanistan would have more influence on Scotland's salience as a target for international terrorism.

UK *Consequences*

Probably the aspect of Scotland's independence of greatest interest to international opinion would be its consequences for the international role of the UK. The UK policy most directly challenged by Scotland's independence would be its nuclear defence policy.

In 1962, at the height of the Cold War, the UK conscripted Scotland as host to elements of the US' strategic nuclear missile submarine force (the US occupied Holy Loch until 1992). In 1968, Scotland's nuclear duties were extended to the provision of base facilities at Faslane for the UK's own submarine-based Polaris missile force. The UK's four nuclear missile submarines continue to be based at Faslane today, with Trident missiles having replaced the Polaris missiles. The UK Government plans to replace the Tridents with a new generation of strategic missiles in 2025, also based at Faslane, and to transfer the balance of the UK's fleet of nuclear submarines there by 2016–17, bringing Scotland's base complement of nuclear submarines to 14 on current commissioning plans.

Hosting the European-based component of the US nuclear strike force and the UK Government's Polaris supplied force put Scotland in the front line of the West's Cold War stand-off with the Soviet Union.

A nuclear war between the Soviet Union and the US and its allies would have been an unimaginable catastrophe not just for those countries but for the whole world. For Scotland as a functioning advanced society, it would have been terminal. The Holy Loch and Faslane facilities are within 25 miles of Glasgow. Half of Scotland's population lived within a 50-mile radius of the bases. In addition to the immediate destruction caused by a nuclear exchange, a prevailing west wind would have doused the central lowlands of Scotland with radioactive fallout. Whatever survived would have been unrecognisable as Scotland.

The UK Government's decision to conscript Scotland in this way was never referred to the Scottish population and no Scottish Parliament existed to pursue the issue. Following the Cuban missile crisis of 1962, it is unlikely that a Scottish Parliament would have consented to the presence of US or any other strategic nuclear submarines in Scottish territory. The total risk – the probability of a deliberate nuclear exchange, or of a nuclear accident, multiplied by the consequences for Scotland – would have been judged too great.

While the probability of nuclear war is very much lower today than in the 1960s, the presence of the UK's nuclear force at Faslane continues to pose a significant risk to Scotland. Those who believe that there is a case on national security grounds for retaining a UK strategic nuclear capability must believe that there remains some risk, however indeterminate, of a deliberate nuclear attack on the UK: why else retain a strategic deterrent? Rather more substantial is the risk of a nuclear accident involving either a nuclear warhead, a submarine's nuclear reactor, or some combination of the two. There is also a constant risk of damage to the regional or local environment from accidental spills and leaks of radiocative material (*Sunday Herald* 2010; *The Guardian*, 2011).[7] Finally there is a risk of terrorist attack against the prime military asset of a state seen by many as the USA's leading collaborator.

In traditional national interest terms, exposing the Scottish population and environment to these risks could be justified only by some conspicuous security benefit to Scotland or to her local and regional allies. In today's conditions it is impossible to identify any such benefit. As we have seen, there is no conventional security threat to Scotland or the rUK in their local or regional theatres. Nor is there any plausible nuclear threat to the UK or to western Europe as a whole. States such as North Korea and Iran suspected of military nuclear ambitions have regional, not global, objectives in mind and the most promising strategies to prevent them from acquiring an operational nuclear capacity involve the application of political and economic pressure in support of regional or global solutions. Meanwhile, the default justification for retaining a nuclear capacity, that no one knows what might happen in the future, is a prescription for endless proliferation.

Quite apart from the dangers to people and environment from the presence in Scotland of the UK's major concentration of nuclear weapons, the maintenance of a UK nuclear strike force incurs heavy opportunity costs. In the conventional analysis the most obvious is the diversion of military expenditure from conventional forces properly equipped for the global war on terror, noted by senior retired military figures such as former Chief of the General Staff Lord Guthrie (*The Guardian*, 2010).[8] From a progressive perspective it is the damage which the UK's nuclear posture inflicts on global efforts to halt the proliferation of nuclear weapons and the waste of resources which could be used to support international development or environmental programmes or other international public goods. From domestic UK and Scottish perspectives it is the diversion of scarce public funds from more productive social and economic investment. Scotland's contribution to the maintenance of the current Trident force within the UK is around £200m a year with a further £2–2.5bn over the next 15 years for the projected Trident replacement.

The UK's nuclear strike force is only one element of the threat posed to Scotland by the military nuclear role assigned to it by the UK Government. In 2010, the UK Ministry of Defence announced that it intended to base all the UK's nuclear powered submarines at Faslane by 2016–17. On current MOD commissioning plans that means that Faslane will become the home base for 14 nuclear-powered submarines – four nuclear missile carrying Vanguard class, three Trafalgar hunter-killer submarines and seven of the newest Astute class multi-role attack submarines armed with non-nuclear Cruise missiles – doubling the complement as it stood in 2011.

Nuclear Risks

This build-up of Scotland's nuclear burden involves an unavoidable increase in the risks. There is the enhanced risk of accidents from the higher levels of submarine movements and increased handling of the submarines in the base facilities. As highly armed combat vessels, the non-nuclear missile submarines could appear tempting targets for terrorist attacks: in addition to their role as escort vessels for the nuclear missile submarines, their Cruise missiles, with a range of up to 1,00 miles can provide support for UK interventions in crisis spots around the world. In November 2011, the MOD acknowledged that non-nuclear missile-carrying submarines from Faslane would be available to support US action against Iran's alleged military nuclear programme (*The Guardian*, 2011).[9]

It was consistent with the UK Government's traditional indifference to Scotland's interests that the MOD failed to carry out a risk assessment before deciding to concentrate the UK's nuclear submarine force in Scotland (MOD, 2011).[10] It is more surprising that the Scottish Government, with its commitment to a non-nuclear Scotland, in both civil and military terms, raised no objection to the decision to base all the UK's nuclear powered submarines at Faslane. Like the MOD it failed to carry out or commission a risk assessment (Scottish Government, 2011).[11] Indeed, in a submission to the UK Basing Review the Scottish Government described the decision as 'welcome' while reiterating its commitment to rid Scotland of nuclear missile submarines (Scottish Government, 2011).[12]

The inconsistency between the Scottish Government's commitment to phase out civil nuclear power on general environmental grounds and its welcome to a prospective doubling of the total of civil and military nuclear reactors using Scottish seas and land was ignored. Taken with the failure of the SNP to date (March 2012) to outline its preferred defence strategy for an independent Scotland and its continuing campaign to maximise the UK's defence presence and expenditure in Scotland, it is difficult to avoid the conclusion that defence is one area where an 'independence-lite' option may be on the agenda of the SNP leadership.

Military Unionism

By extension, independence-lite poses a threat to the SNP's traditional commitment to expel nuclear missiles from Scotland. If independence campaigners were to present themselves as desperate to retain the jobs and income provided by a major UK defence presence in Scotland, including capital defence contracts supporting several thousands of jobs at Govan and Scotstoun in the west and at Rosyth in the east, they would be inviting the response from the UK Government – 'You can have our defence jobs and contracts if you provide a base for our nuclear submarines but you cannot have the one without the other.'

It also exposes an independent Scotland to a demand that if it wanted to retain rUK military resources and service and defence industry jobs in Scotland then it should be willing to help pay for them. That would reduce the size of the savings that Scotland could expect to make by moving from a high cost UK defence strategy to a moderate cost Nordic defence strategy. And the difference could be substantial. As noted in the Economic Case, an independent Scotland would be in a position to reduce its defence expenditure to Norwegian levels, releasing at least £1.1bn for alternative uses.

Challenge to UK Status

If the champions of independence retained their traditional non-nuclear stance, independence would present a serious and probably unanswerable challenge to the continuation of the UK as a nuclear power. Whatever the doubts raised by the ambiguity of SNP policy on UK military bases, the SNP Government insists that it has a non-negotiable commitment to the removal of nuclear missiles from Scotland. Even without an SNP Government, the parliament of an independent Scotland would be likely to find the risks from the presence in Scotland of the rUK's sole nuclear base unacceptable, not least because as a separate country Scotland would have even less control over the rUK's nuclear decisions than as part of the UK. Majorities of both Scottish MPs and MSPs have voted against the Trident renewal proposals reflecting the views of major institutions of Scottish civil society such as the churches and the STUC (BBC *News Challenge*, 2007).[13]

In the face of this Scottish fiat, the challenge for the rUK Government would be to find a site on the rUK coast offering both the physical and locational advantages of Faslane, including its distance from London and the south-east. Even if such a site could be found local opposition would be strong and in the post-Cold War era would be shared by a large section of the rUK public faced with the £billions costs of constructing and equipping the base over and above the £25bn cost of the Trident renewal programme. Scottish independence could finally force the end of the UK's military nuclear role (Chalmers and Walker, 2001).[14]

Surrendering the UK's membership of the nuclear club would be a bitter pill for the UK's political establishment. The UK deterrent is valued by the London political establishment as much as a support to global power status than for its military value. In his memoir, *A Journey,* Tony Blair reveals that he could see the 'force of the common sense and practical argument against Trident but giving it up would be too big a downgrading of our status as a nation' (Blair, 2010).[15]

By itself, Scotland's withdrawal from the Union might encourage questions about the UK's international status. If it was followed by unilateral nuclear disarmament these questions could crystallise into calls for a review of the rUK's permanent membership of the UN Security Council, though many in the UN would be reluctant to strengthen the perception of a link between the possession of nuclear weapons and Council membership. More likely such calls would strengthen the case for diluting the power of the original four permanent members – the US, Russia as the successor to the Soviet Union, the UK and France – by the addition of new members such as India, Germany and Japan or of the Security Council collectively by reinforcing the status of the General Assembly.

Anticipating such calls, the rUK's political establishment might try to protect its status by accommodating a nuclear strike force, whatever the political or economic cost, on the coast of England or Wales. But the public in the rUK might consider that their interests would be better served by receiving a Scottish decision to expel nuclear weapons from Scotland as the final curtain on the UK's global power ambitions and throwing the rUK's weight behind a global campaign against nuclear proliferation (Johnston *et al.*, 2006).[16]

Other international consequences of Scotland's independence would be modest by comparison. An independent Scotland would be likely to conform to the foreign policy dynamic of small countries. It could be expected to adopt the adage that policy should always be the first line of defence and apply a higher threshold of legality and UN endorsement to its participation in international military interventions than the UK. (The Scottish Parliament's refusal in January 2003 to support the SNP, the Greens and the SSP in condemning the UK Government's plans to invade Iraq probably had more to do with Labour MSPs' loyalty to a UK Labour Government than to their own convictions).

Scottish opinion has generally been more favourable to EU membership than UK opinion though support has suffered from the eurozone crisis. It is likely that Scotland's policy on the EU would be pragmatic, probably sharing the UK's preference for a confederal rather than federal future for the Union. As its main trading partner, the rUK would continue to exert a major influence particularly on currency arrangements, the more so because of the euro crisis. Scotland would have every reason to seek to balance the influence of the rUK by cultivating close relationships with selected European neighbours, notably the Nordic states with their pragmatic approach to the future of the EU. On reform of the UN and other international institutions, an independent Scotland could be expected to give greater weight to the claims of smaller countries than the UK with its 'great power' pretensions has done.

There appears to be a more active sympathy in Scotland than south of the border for a clutch of progressive international causes – Palestinian statehood, more humane treatment for asylum seekers, a more liberal immigration policy – but how far this would influence policy under independence is difficult to judge. On development aid and global trade Scotland's position would probably be broadly similar to that of the rUK in its current liberal mode. Its position on international financial regulation on the other hand would depend on fundamental choices to be made between a neo-liberal or a social democratic future for Scotland.

Conclusion

An independent Scotland would enjoy an unusually benign security environment within its immediate region. Globally the spread of intergovernmental institutions has increased the opportunities for small countries to represent themselves on the world stage and Scotland has interests sufficiently distinct from those of the UK – on defence, marine resources, energy, climate change, social vision, and some diplomatic issues – to benefit from those opportunities.

Scotland's place in Europe would remain to be determined as the main features of the EU after the euro crisis became clear. The strong probability is that the response of the EU to a Scottish bid for membership would be taken not on technical legal grounds or on the grounds of existing members' internal constitutional interests but by the EU's established criteria and practice.

While the eurozone fiscal pact would constrain Scotland's economic freedom more tightly than other currency options, her relative fiscal strength would align her more closely with the 'northern core' than the peripheral states of the Mediterranean and Ireland, securing a significant degree of fiscal flexibility. She would be able to make her own decisions on participation in collective security arrangements and in joint interventions such as Iraq and Afghanistan with all their political, moral and financial ramifications.

Meanwhile, by rejecting a role in the UK's nuclear strategy, Scotland could promote both her own security and contribute to global efforts to prevent nuclear proliferation. A significant secondary benefit would be the increase in the knowledge and awareness of global developments which Scotland could expect from her direct participation in global governance.

References

1 Paterson, L, *The Autonomy of Modern Scotland*. Edinburgh University Press, 1994; MacCormick, N, *Questioning Sovereignty*. Oxford University Press, 1999; Keating, M, *The Independence of Scotland*. Oxford University Press, 2009.

2 Maxwell, S, 'Politics' in Carty, T and McCall-Smith, A (eds), *Power and Manoeuverability: The International Implications of an Independent Scotland*. Edinburgh, 1977.

3 Commission on Scottish Devolution, *Serving Scotland Better: Scotland and the United Kingdom in the 21st Century*. HMG, 2009.

4 Steel Commission, *Moving to Federalism: A New Settlement for Scotland*. Scottish Liberal Democrats, Edinburgh, 2006.

5 Murkens, J et al. *Scottish Independence: Legal and Constitutional Issues: A Practical Guide*. Edinburgh University Press, 2002; House of Commons

Library, Note 6110 Scotland, independence and the EU. House of Commons, 2011.

6 García-Margallo JM. *The Scotsman*, 27.02 2012.

7 *Sunday Herald*, 16/05/2010; *The Guardian* 20/04/2009, 26/08/2011.

8 Guthrie, C, *The Guardian*, 10/03/2010.

9 *The Guardian*, 2/11/2011.

10 Reply to Freedom of Information request to the Ministry of Defence, 15/08/2011.

11 Reply to a Freedom of Information request to the Scottish Government, August 2011.

12 *Submission to the UK Basing Review*. Scottish Government, June 2011.

13 *Scottish MPs and MSPs oppose Trident replacement*. BBC *News Challenge* website, 14/06/2007

14 Chalmers, M and Walker, W, *Uncharted Waters: The UK, Nuclear Weapons and the Scottish Question*. East Linton, 2000.

15 Blair, T, *A Journey*. London, 2010.

16 Johnston, R *et al.* (eds) *Worse Than Irrelevant? British Nuclear Weapons in the 21st Century*. Acronym Institute for Disarmament and Diplomacy, London, 2006.

The Cultural Case

Introduction

A CULTURAL CASE for independence is not the same as cultural nationalism. Cultural nationalism is the promotion of a particular cultural tradition held to define a national identity. The romantic nationalism of 19th century Europe usually located that culture in a distinctive language which was typically scorned as provincial and socially inferior by the imperial centre when it was not being actively suppressed. Scotland's vulnerability to external pressure – from the Reformation in the 16th century and the loss of the Scottish Court in 1603 and of Scotland's Parliament a century later, to the steady erosion of Scotland's surviving institutions of civil society by empire, industrialisation and mass communications – meant that Scotland provided barren ground for the growth of a cohesive linguistically-based culture capable of carrying a sense of national identity. In 'A Drunk Man Looks at the Thistle', MacDiarmid mocked his impossible legacy as a Scottish poet and cultural nationalist: 'In this heterogeneous hotch and rabble, Why am I condemned to squabble?' before stoically concluding, 'A Scottish poet maun assume / The burden o' his people's doom / And dee to brak their living tomb' (MacDiarmid, 1962).[1]

MacDiarmid's linguistic revivalism has not been the only cultural strategy for national revival on offer to modern Scotland. The prospects for the revival of the Scottish tradition of democratic intellectualism as described in George Davie's *The Democratic Intellect* and *The Crisis of the Democratic Intellect* have been a recurring reference in subsequent debates on Scotland's cultural future (Davie, 1961; 1968).[2] But following the failure of MacDiarmid's linguistic revivalism to generate a national revival, the failure of Davie's democratic intellectualism to exert any significant leverage on the development of Scottish education suggests that, for better or worse, interpretations or reinventions of distinctive cultural traditions – whatever their strengths – are too narrow to carry the complex identity of modern Scotland. The renaissance of Scottish arts in the 1980s, provoked in some accounts by frustration at the failure of the movement for devolution in the 1970s and represented in fiction by such writers as Alasdair Gray, James Kelman, Irvine Welsh, Janice Galloway, Iain Banks and others, was more concerned with exploring individual, often iconoclastic, visions of Scotland than with perpetuating or reinventing a specific Scottish tradition or identity. The spread of the digital culture from the 1990s, bringing with it new creative possibilities which subverted traditional categories of artist, audience and place, has added to the fragmentation. In this new environment, a cultural case for Scotland's independence needs to demonstrate that independence can improve the environment for whatever forms of cultural activity Scots choose to pursue and whatever their relationship to traditional understandings of Scotland's identity.

Arts Under Devolution

Post-crisis funding anxieties apart, the creative arts in Scotland are generally considered to be in good health. A recent assessment by one of Scotland's best-known cultural critics, Joyce McMillan, goes further. McMillan affirms the power of the arts in Scotland 'to transform Scotland's view of itself – to reframe the nation not as a problematic provincial backwater but as a powerhouse of 21st-century creativity, generating work that is recognised on a global level for its ability to articulate the current human condition.' And she is clear that the achievements of the Scottish arts today are due in large measure to the contribution of public policy over several decades. She sums up the estimated £300m annual public investment the Scottish arts receive 'as the best, the brightest, and the most brilliantly cost-effective the government of any small nation could make' (McMillan, 2010).[3] Against such a positive assessment what could independence contribute to their further improvement?

McMillan may be a little too enthusiastic. While the visual arts, music and drama flourish and the strengths of Scottish poetry and fiction are widely acknowledged, other arts, such as architecture, dance and film, struggle to achieve comparable recognition and, despite some notable individual successes, publishing in Scotland continues to struggle.

While cultural policy under independence would continue to be influenced by much the same considerations as under devolution, some areas would be likely to command priority. Broadcasting is the obvious case. No developed independent country would tolerate the poor representation of its national life which Scotland currently receives from the BBC and the commercial broadcasters. The Scottish Parliament unanimously agreed the recommendations of the Scottish Commission on Broadcasting for a Scottish Digital Network providing a public service network and an online hub costing 2% of the BBC's annual income from its licence fee. (Commission on Scottish Broadcasting, 2009).[4] But under devolution, broadcasting is a reserved responsibility and, notwithstanding the precedent of the Welsh language channel SC4, the views of the Commission and the Scottish Parliament left the UK's broadcasters and policy makers largely unmoved.

If independence would be likely to lead to the development of a public service Scottish broadcasting channel, securing the future of the Scottish printed media would prove more difficult. Contrary to expectation, political devolution failed to stimulate a recovery of Scottish-produced newspapers in the face of the challenge of London-based papers and of the growth of the internet, and periodical publishing is at a particularly low ebb. Most countries provide VAT relief for their press and Norway provides a modest newsprint subsidy for minority papers. In many ways, a prior problem for the Scottish press is its ownership structure, but when the internet is threatening the long-term future of the printed press, the prospect of finding Scottish bidders to buy out the existing owners is fanciful. One option, at least in the medium term, is the idea of publicly endowed journalists' trusts or cooperatives based on the internet. But independence would be more likely to highlight the challenge of securing a diverse, Scottish-based media, digital or printed, than to reveal easy solutions.

Nor can we assume that independence would seamlessly fill the gaps in the arts in Scotland, creating a vibrant film industry, a flourishing dance scene, a dynamic architecture and a world-beating publishing and video games sector. Whatever else independence will provide, it should not be expected to conjure up either the money or the personnel to challenge London's dominance in these and other areas of the arts. If London's own promotional agencies are to be believed, one in every eight people in London works in a 'creative industry' and with just 12% of the UK's population London provides one third of all the UK's 'creative jobs', with the south east providing another 26%. London is particularly dominant in radio and TV with three and half times its share of jobs (prior to the BBC's partial migration to Salford) as well as in publishing, advertising and film and video where it has two and half times its population share. The most frequently cited analyst of London's cultural role speaks of the 'intimate links' between the creative industries and the city's financial and business sectors, noting that 53% of the demand for London's creative output comes from these sectors (Freeman, 2008).[5]

While London's public arts institutions, led by the National Galleries and Museums and the national performing arts bodies such as the Royal Opera and the National Theatre, are not included as creative industries, their role in assuring London's cultural dominance is critical. They enjoy privileged access not only to public funding but also to the commercial sector's sponsorship of the arts. Despite a 30% cut in the Arts Council of England's total budget, London arts organisations secured 49% of the Council's grants for 2011, some £510m. while in 2010 businesses contributed no less than £73m to London arts' organisations, estimated at 68% of the total business support for the arts in the UK. (*London Evening Standard*, 2011; London Loves Business, 2011).[6,7] These figures do not include the financial support by private benefactors, much of it tax privileged, which is overwhelmingly concentrated in London, nor the £90m of public money for the two year long Cultural Olympiad, of which over 50% is destined for the 10-week London Festival 2012.

There is little Scotland can do to challenge this concentration of financial and cultural power in one corner of the British Isles except to stop feeding London's conceit by allowing it to govern Scotland's territory and population with whatever portion of political and cultural prestige and tax revenues they supply.

Politics as Culture

In a democracy, politics provides society with the most accessible form of that dialogue with itself and the wider world which is the heart of a culture. A vigorous politics, intellectually and morally equipped to identify and analyse the key challenges of the present day and to develop feasible responses, is essential to a healthy culture.

Without independence, Scots cannot feel fully responsible for their own future and for what they can do for the world, for the simple reason that they are not fully responsible. By surrendering their right to decide such fundamental questions as the extent of inequality they accept in their society, or whether their land should be used as a base for weapons of mass destruction, or whether they should send fellow citizens to kill and be killed in military interventions in Iraq or Afghanistan, they are accepting a division between thought and action which weakens and corrupts Scotland's public culture.

Unionists will respond that this argument is circular because the claim for these debilitating effects assumes that the sense of identity Scots apply to such fundamental questions is Scottish rather than British – when in fact the majority of Scots, while calling themsleves more Scottish than British, appear content to contribute their opinions on such issues to a process of decision-taking at UK level rather than insist on decisions being taken in Scotland. Thus as far as high level political decisions are concerned, their moral community is the UK, not Scotland. And they can make a plausible appeal to the historical record. The greatest modern Scottish contributions to world culture – the Scottish Enlightenment of the first half of the 18th century and its Indian summer in the first half of the 19th century – happened under the Union.

But there are some critical qualifications to be entered. During those years of outstanding Scottish intellectual achievement between 1740 and 1850, Britain was the world's most dynamic society and became the dominant world power. If the Scottish response to the stimulus this provided was particularly vigorous it was in part because Scotland was able to draw on the distinctive achievements of pre-Union Scotland, notably in education, a more democratic national church and a distinctive legal system whose autonomy was believed to be protected by the Union settlement. The contrast with today is obvious. In its long decline from empire the UK has lost that general confidence in the superiority of its public institutions which was one of the sources of its intellectual energy, and London's evident self-satisfaction with its role as a global city is no substitute. Meanwhile, the autonomy which Scotland's institutions were promised by the Union proved a diminishing asset as their dominance in Scottish life was challenged by the growth of UK-wide institutions such as business corporations and trade unions, the central British state in its proliferating roles, and mass media increasingly directed from London. Where the Union was once experienced by many Scots as empowering and stimulating, as the 20th century progressed it began to be felt as constricting and debilitating.

Moral Autonomy

Despite their political loyalty to the Union, most Unionists agree that Scotland is a nation in some sense beyond the merely sentimental. Defining national identity has always been difficult and has become especially so in the multicultural societies of a globalising world. But one underrated dimension of the Scots' complex sense of nationality is the idea of Scotland as a moral community. That sense of moral community is most widely attached to established Scottish myths of egalitarianism, or of Scotland as a more socially compassionate country than England, or of Scotland as less racially prejudiced and more welcoming to migrants and asylum seekers. The durability of such self-congratulatory representations may draw on a persisting belief with roots deep in Scotland's history that Scotland constitutes an autonomous moral community with a capacity and a responsibility to determine its own stance on the most fundamental issues facing humankind. In this perspective Scotland is most identifiably 'in character' when debating the big moral issues of the day – the Church of Scotland's General Assembly pronouncing on the ethics of markets, the Catholic bishops condemning weapons of mass destruction, the STUC demanding a Living Wage as part of a campaign against growing inequality, the voluntary sector rallying to Make Poverty History, the Scottish Parliament voting against the replacement of Trident and in support of Palestinian rights.

This sense of Scotland as an autonomous moral community was made unusually explicit in August 2009 when Scottish Justice Secretary Kenny MacAskill used his discretionary power to release the convicted Lockerbie mass murderer Abdelbaset Ali Mohmed al-Megrahi from his Scottish prison on compassionate grounds because of a diagnosis of terminal cancer. MacAskill justified his decision by insisting that it was consistent with the provisions of Scots law and its underpinning values.

Some people in Scotland, and many more in the UK and the US, disagreed with MacAskill's decision, but few in Scotland questioned the decision with all its international ramifications being taken in Scotland. Margo MacDonald's Assisted Dying (Scotland) Bill in the 2007 Scottish Parliament dealt with an equally fundamental and complex moral issue. Again, the proposition it promotes is controversial in Scotland as elsewhere, but no challenge has been raised on constitutional or other grounds to Scotland's right to debate and determine the issue for itself.

In a submission to the Commission on Scottish Devolution, Professor John Haldane urged the Commissioners to give serious attention to the question of Scotland's 'moral autonomy', describing it as 'more fundamental and more extensive' than the question of fiscal autonomy (Commission on Scottish Devolution, 2008).[8] His particular focus was a clause in Westminster's Human Fertilisation and Embryology Bill giving the UK Health Minister wide discretion to permit radical departures from the specified powers without public consultation but he posed a wider question. 'If education and social services are not reserved [to Westminster], why should broadcasting, abortion, human fertilisation and other matters bearing directly on moral values not also be devolved?' Or, many would add, war and peace, social justice and the Scottish contribution to international development?

Moral Autonomy and Political Authority

A presumption that Scotland possesses 'moral autonomy' is barely compatible with any devolved or even federal division of powers between Holyrood and Westminster. Such limits on Scotland's moral autonomy might be justified by some compelling pragmatic reason for sharing decision taking with Westminster, though it would be subject always to a conscientious exemption. Compelling pragmatic reasons for conceding moral autonomy are harder to find than they used to be. The UK's relative economic decline has undermined the plausibility of the economic case against independence just as the political case against has been challenged by the widespread acceptance of the principle of devolution as a continuing process. The moral authority of metropolitan UK has been diminished by the erosion of Britain's civil liberties under New Labour and by the longer term discrediting of the

Westminster model of government. The call for Scotland to 'lead the way' has become a feature of policy debates in devolved Scotland, from free care for the elderly, the ending of student tuition fees and electoral reform, to the Climate Change (Scotland) Act 2009, the ending of the Right to Buy for new social housing and the campaign for a minimum unit price for alcohol.

Impending developments in the mainstream of public policy are likely to increase the sense of moral difference north and south of the border. The modest bias of Scottish public opinion in favour of the public provision of welfare was transformed by the political dynamics of the first decade of devolution into a significant divergence of policy in key social policy areas between the England and Scotland. The Calman Report seeks to justify the Unionist premise on which its recommendations are built by appealing to the existence of a 'social union' at UK level described as a 'common understanding between the Parliaments in the Union about the services that constitute the welfare state – the most important of which will be health care, care for the elderly and education – and on what basis they are supplied – substantially free at the point of need' and cites the existence of a statement of principles for the NHS across the UK (Commission on Scottish Devolution 2009).[9] The policy of the UK Conservative–Liberal Democrat Government in subordinating the provision of welfare state to the logic of the market and extending the market in health and education in England well beyond New Labour's reforms threatens to transform an evolving divergence into a parting of the ways on a scale to justify Haldane's suggestion of a historic tension between 'Scottish welfare communitarianism' and 'English liberal individualism' (Haldane, 2008).[10]

Obstacles

If there is a persisting expectation on the part of the Scottish public that Scotland should conduct itself as an autonomous moral community there is also a major obstacle. The representative Scottish institutions which most consistently debate the moral dimension of public policy issues – the churches, the STUC, the political parties, the voluntary sector, the media – continue, explicitly or by default, to endorse political Union. None of them supports their moralising rhetoric with a claim for the Scottish community to have the same collective power to act on its conclusions that other moral communities enjoy through political independence. Rather, in respect of many of their of their most critical moral determinations, these Scottish forums of Scottish opinion are limited to urging agencies outwith Scotland, and with only attenuated accountability to Scotland, to act on Scotland's behalf.

Devolution goes some way to correcting this gap between moralising and active responsibility but not very far. Quite apart from the reservation to Westminster of the classic moral issues, from war to abortion, the fiscal crisis demonstrates how little protection the current division of powers affords. Decisions made in London on the rate, depth and priorities of UK spending cuts affect Scotland right across the spectrum of devolved areas. What price Scotland's welfare communitarianism when England is intent on the economics of retrenchment? Even the most radical forms of devolution would leave London with power to determine Scotland's responses to the most fundamental moral choices of war and peace as well as the big issues of global politics.

The gap between the moralising rhetoric common in Scottish public life and widespread acceptance of an inability to act on it in key areas is one likely source of the cynicism and inertia which continues to mark Scottish public life. The recent record offers some particularly egregious examples. The Scottish Constitutional Convention's 1989 *Claim of Right for Scotland* asserted the sovereign right of the Scottish people to choose their own future. It was subscribed to by leaders of the Labour Party and the Scottish Liberal Democrats as a founding principle of the devolution settlement. But those parties casually repudiated the spirit of the *Claim*, if not its letter, by blocking moves in the 2007–11 Parliament for a popular referendum on Scotland's constitutional future and in 2012 by challenging the Scottish Parliament's right to decide the terms of a referendum on independence.

The Labour Party has for decades been adept at exploiting the gap between the rhetoric of moral denunciation and Scotland's power to act. Its traditional – though by no means unanimous – response in Scotland to the existence of UK Governments with programmes hostile to the Scottish majority values, including Labour Governments intent on extending market forces within the NHS, has been to offer itself as the champion of Scottish interests against the failings of London Governments as if its own commitment to preserving the Union had nothing to do with the matter. Since Labour's ejection from government at West-minster in the 2010 UK election, Scottish Labour has again attempted to present itself as Scotland's champion against expenditure cuts while pinning the blame on the Scottish Government, despite a Labour Government having established the Scottish Parliament as a spending authority overwhelmingly dependent on Westminster for its funding, and their own Chancellor Alistair Darling's pre-election warning that under a new Labour Government the cuts 'would be worse than Thatcher's'.

The rhetoric of resistance, Scottish Labour calculates, will always trump the facts. The institution which most comfortably inhabits Scotland's gap between rhetoric and responsibility is also the Scottish institution most intimate with corruption, whether the petty corruption of invented expenses' claims and local patronage or of former First Minister Jack McConnell's taking the ermine on the grounds that membership of the House of Lords would allow him to pursue his lifelong commitment to egalitarianism.

By equipping Scots with the authority and responsibility to act across the whole spectrum of issues, independence would expose Scotland's moralising rhetoric of resistance to sterner tests than it will ever face under the forms of devolution currently touted by the Unionist parties. It would remove the alibi for inaction provided by the Union and confront the voters with the consequences of their collusion in the politicians' rhetoric.

How much would we be prepared to pay in higher taxes for our opposition to spending cuts? How many more asylum seekers or economic migrants would we be ready to welcome to Scotland when the UK Border Agency is no longer there to do the dirty work of control and deportation? How much redistribution of income and wealth are the better off prepared to accept in the name of a fairer and more compassionate Scotland? How many jobs are we prepared to jeopardise in the short term as the price of terminating our role in the UK's delusional defence strategy?

The answers might be unsettling, but our public culture would be the better for being able to subject politicians' rhetoric to the test of practical responsibility.

A Cultural Consequence?

Scottish culture is open to a more general weakness that may also have its roots in the limitations on Scotland's power of collective determination and action. For the last several decades, the mainstream of the Scottish creative arts have failed to connect consistently with the political and public dramas of their own society. Even such acknowledged stars of Scotland's cultural scene as theatre and fiction have fallen short. It is most obvious in the threadbare history of political theatre in Scotland though it goes well beyond that rather problematic form. Comparisons with English culture, especially when accessed through the self-promoting lens of the London media, are risky but over the last three decades England seems to have enjoyed at least a silver age of political theatre provoked by the rise and fall of Thatcherism and New Labour. One thinks of Hare, Edgar, Churchill, Ravenhill, Stenham and Prebble. The same could not be claimed for Scotland. London-based expatriates Alistair Beaton and Armando Ianucci have contributed their TV satires of New Labour, but since the demise of John McGrath's 7:84 in the 1980s and its various spin-offs, only Gregory Burke and David Greig have achieved any public profile for their treatment of Scottish public themes.

The causes are more likely to lie in Scotland's wider public culture than in Scottish policy for the arts. There are after all Scottish dramatists who write with a clear social or political interest to put alongside Greig and Burke – Henry Adams, Douglas Maxwell and Cora Bissett, for example. But their work seems to struggle for wider audiences and publicity beyond the brief spotlight of an Edinburgh Festival award or a review in a specialist journal. Which brings us back to the disjunction between the moralising rhetoric of public life and the limited contribution which Scotland's stunted political culture is able to make to the reimagining of Scotland.

In the era of confident empire centred in London, such an imbalance was unsurprising. But Scotland's experience of change over the last three decades has been no less fateful than England's. In its resistance to Thatcherism and its growing divergence from the British political norm, in the long struggle for dominance between Labour and the SNP, in its puzzling acquiescence to London's manoeuvres to retain monopoly control over Scotland's North Sea oil revenues, in the political tangle of the al-Megrahi affair, in the whole overarching struggle for a self-determining future after empire, Scotland's story surely offers as much moral drama for those who live here as the English or British story told by London-based writers.

Yet Scotland's dramatists, and indeed her novelists and filmmakers too, have mostly been unable or disinclined, to represent this drama convincingly to their own public. While the novels of Alasdair Gray, James Kelman, Irvine Welsh and Andrew Greig reference political themes, James Robertson is the only contemporary Scottish writer to have put the dramas of Scotland's public life at the centre of a novel (*And the Land Lay Still*) in the way that Ian McEwan, Martin Amis, Julian Barnes, John Le Carré, Alan Hollinghurst and other English novelists – not to mention the current crop of 'London' novels, represented most prominently by John Lanchester – weave the moral dramas of British public life into the experiences of their characters (Robertson, 2010; *The Observer*, 27/02/2012).[11]

Some fields of creative writing not conventionally considered as within the mainstream escape this generalisation: Scottish historical writing and cultural analysis have blossomed in response to the stirrings of literary and political nationalism, and historical writing embracing a range of views on the national question continues to go from strength to strength. But – to skip media – in recent decades the mainstream of Scottish creative writing has failed to produce a *Borgen* moment. The Danish television's series centred on the political and personal triumphs and trials of a Danish female Prime Minister demonstrates that the public life of small countries are not predestined to dullness.

In *Scott and Scotland: The Predicament of the Scottish Writer* (1936), Edwin Muir proclaimed that the dissociation of thought and feeling which he believed was the fate of Scott as of every Scottish writer since the Reformation, was because Scott lived in 'a hiatus, in a country, that is to say, which was neither a nation nor a province, but had instead of a centre, a blank, an Edinburgh, in the middle of it' (Muir, 1982).[12]

In his Introduction to the 1982 edition, Allan Massie highlights the perversity of Muir's denial of the historical fact that Scotland was a nation, altogether ignoring the fact that Scotland was a nation without a state. But instead of exploring what influence Muir's blindness on this crucial point might have had on his understanding of the predicament of the Scottish writer, Massie extends Muir's thesis: 'Our condition has worsened since Muir wrote and our condition is certainly worse than Scott's was... Scott's Scotland retained a public life: ours has none. The writer thus lives in a society which has abandoned responsibility for its own direction... and which finds that whole sectors of it do no more than reflect a way of life that is lived more intensely and urgently elsewhere' (Massie, 1982).[13]

Although Massie was writing as a Unionist, it is difficult not to sense in his pessimism the shadow of the failure of the 1979 Assembly referendum, evident again in the only one of of his many novels which treats of contemporary Scottish Nationalism, *One Night In Winter*. (Massie, 1984).[14] But ever the realist, Massie (still a Unionist) was writing 12 years later: 'There are still those who would rather be in the last ditch, denying realities rather than submit to them... I expect the last ditch to be a crowded place, littered with Unionist corpses, honourably dead of course, but very dead' (Massie, 1994).

Seventeen years on again, Massie might concede that the 'blank' at the centre of Scottish life – Edinburgh as the cold symbol of Scotland's soul – has begun to fill up with a deal more writing, acting, arguing, singing and dancing, painting and exhibition-making and general craic about Scotland and its place in a turbulent world than any respectable hiatus could be expected to accommodate.

Conclusion

Independence would eliminate the gap between Scotland's instinct for moral autonomy and its inability to act on its moral conclusions. By establishing Scotland as a place where the most fundamental issues had to be confronted and responses decided, it would strengthen the role of Scottish politics in the evolving drama of Scottish life and help fill that 'blank' at the heart of Scotland which Muir found so enervating. By raising the stakes in Scottish public life, it would identify an audience for those writers and other artists keen to explore the changing political and moral context of Scottish experience.

By formally withdrawing Scotland from British control, independence would erode London's claim to speak for a British identity, and by amplifying Scotland's voice, strengthen the prospects for a more differentiated cultural life within the British Isles.

By engaging Scotland directly in international developments, independence would also raise awareness of global issues. It would increase pressure on the Scottish media, wherever and however they were owned, to improve their coverage of Scottish public life. It could be expected to encourage increased support at the least to those national cultural institutions which most independent countries consider vital to the health of their culture, including a public broadcasting service. And in response to the heightened national awareness, it could be expected to extend support for the Scots language alongside Gaelic and strengthen the Scottish content of education – for example, by requiring more Scottish history and literature to be taught in schools – all in the cause of supporting a confidently diverse and eclectic Scottish culture.

References

1 MacDiarmid, H, 'A Drunk Man Looks at the Thistle' in *The Collected Poems of Hugh MacDiarmid*, Edinburgh, 1962.

2 Davie, G, *The Democratic Intellect: Scotland and her Universities in the Nineteenth Century.* Edinburgh University Press, 1961; *The Crisis of the Democratic Intellect.* Edinburgh University Press, 1968.

3 McMillan, J, 'Arts budget hardly deserves to "share the pain" of the country's cuts'. *The Scotsman*, 24/07/2010.

4 *Platform for Success.* Scottish Government Commission on Scottish Broadcasting, 2009.

5 Freeman, A, *London: A Cultural Audit.* Greater London Economics, 2008.

6 *London Evening Standard*, 31/03/2011.

7 'Will Business Rescue London's Art Scene?'. London Loves Business website, 13/10/2011.

8 Haldane, J, *Submission to Commission on Scottish Devolution.* Commission website, 2008.

9 Commission on Scottish Devolution, 2009.

10 Haldane, J, 2008.

11 Robertson, J, *And the Land Lay Still*. London, 2010; Preston, A, 'Follow the

Money Back to Trollope', *The Observer*, 27/02/2012.

12 Muir, E, *Scott and Scotland: The Predicament of the Scottish Writer.* Edinburgh, 1982.

13 Massie, A, quoted in Muir, E, *Scott and Scotland: The Predicament of the Scottish Writer.* Edinburgh, 1982.

14 Massie, A, *One Night in Winter*, 1984.

The Environmental Case

Introduction

THE ENVIRONMENTAL CASE for independence is even less developed in the public debate than the arguments on democratic and social grounds. There are a number of reasons for this. In public debate global sustainability is a relatively novel issue which challenges traditional political affiliations. It is also a highly technical field with the opposing sides on the big controversies – global warming, nuclear power or renewables, peak oil – offering levels of statistics or factoids sufficient to silence all but the most recklessly opinionated members of the public. It is not surprising that when the public is asked to choose between specific policies to meet the challenge of global warming rather than just to express a position on the general challenge, their responses are confused.

At the same time, particular features of the Scottish political scene have encouraged a more radical approach to environmental policy in Scotland than in the UK. One influence has been the strength of the anti-nuclear movement in Scotland. The movement outlived its origins in sixties' opposition to the establishment of Faslane as the UK's base for the Polaris nuclear missile submarines to join a new generation opposed to the building at Torness, between 1980 and 1988, of Scotland's sole representative of a second generation of UK nuclear power stations. That opposition was stimulated by widespread reports of Scotland's exposure to the fallout from the Chernobyl disaster in 1986.

The political controversy attached to Scotland's 30-year history as a major oil producer has made Scottish public opinion better informed of the politics and the economics of energy production than opinion in the UK as a whole. The credit for this is due largely to the SNP, which for much of the 1970s was the principal source of analysis of North Sea oil developments for the media and the interested public (Harvie,

1994).[1] The SNP's belief that Westminster had denied Scotland access in the closing decades of the 20th century to the potential long-term benefits of its North Sea oil legacy, including the reinvestment of a share of the oil revenues in the first generation of alternative energies, strengthened its determination to secure a leading role for Scotland in the global drive for renewable energy in the 21st century.

That determination has been fuelled by a growing awareness of Scotland's potential for alternative energy as publicised by the SNP Government – a quarter of Europe's capacity for generating energy from offshore wind and tide and one-tenth of Europe's wave power capacity – and the claims that the economic benefits of successfully developing that capacity could amount to 130,000 jobs in Scotland's low carbon economy, including 26,000 in renewables (Scottish Government, 2010).[2] These factors combined to secure unanimous support in the Scottish Parliament for the ambitious Climate Change Act 2009 which included a mandatory target for a reduction of net carbon emissions of at least 42% by 2020 and at least 80% by 2050 (Scottish Parliament, 2009).[3]

Scotland's 30 years of involvement in oil production had meanwhile created a significant base of expertise in energy production and marine engineering from which to launch a bid to catch up with such pioneers as Norway, Denmark and Germany in the development of a second generation of alternative energy technologies.

Despite the unanimous support in the Scottish Parliament for the Climate Change Act, the Scottish Government's ambitions for reviving the Scottish economy through a renewables revolution is highly contentious. Opposition from the local communities directly affected by wind turbines and transmission pylons, from rural user groups such as the Ramblers Association and some conservation groups, was predictable. The wider environmental movement has generally been more supportive. But as the scale of the proposed renewables revolution has become clear the criticisms have broadened.

One argument is based on claimed shortfalls on the supply side of renewables, including skilled engineers, manufacturing capacity, transmission infrastructure and the capacity of the renewable technologies themselves (Institution of Mechanical Engineers, 2011).[4] The size of the capital requirement, estimated at £46bn, and the potential cost to the Scottish consumer and taxpayer in the event of independence at up to

£4bn depending on how the cost would be divided between the Scottish and rUK consumers, are other areas of contention. (Citibank, November 2011).[5] Yet another, less discussed risk, is the possibility that new discoveries of fossil fuels or an unanticipated technological breakthrough will drive the world energy prices below the level at which governments will feel able to justify the cost of the current generation of renewables to their own electorates.

In the face of these uncertainties, the case for Scotland's renewables strategy rests on four judgements – that the prospect of global warming will continue to drive political demand for low carbon energy; that the price of fossil fuels will continue on an upward trend in response to rising demand from rapidly industrialising economies with large populations; that the relative price of renewables will fall as their technologies mature; and that the nuclear option will continue to be suspect because of public concern over safety along with governments' concerns over the total costs including insurance, waste disposal and dismantling. These factors create the opportunity for Scotland to exploit her comparative natural advantages, including good coastal locations for the manufacturing and supply functions as well as the engineering skills from the oil and gas industry. As Donald Mackay observes, the position with renewables today is not dissimilar to the position of the embryonic North Sea oil and gas industries in the UK and Norway in the late 1960s – a natural resource base of uncertain size requiring massive technological advances to drive down its costs and massive investment to deliver the output to its markets (Mackay, 2011).[6] But with North Sea oil revenues as one source of back-up funding, the medium and long-term odds are too attractive to ignore.

An Independence Bonus?

What would independence add to this combination of social attitudes and natural assets to support a positive Scottish response to the challenges of global warming?

It would be encouraging to think that taking power over the main policy areas influencing Scotland's environment would increase Scots' sense of responsibility for their own environment. But that is not guaranteed. Scots may boast of the beauty of the 'Land of the Mountain and the Flood' but compared with many other European populations they are separated from the land by four or five generations of industrialisation and urban living and unlike their Nordic counterparts few have a family retreat in the country for weekends and summer holidays.

The difference is revealed in the respective Scottish and Nordic attitudes towards their fishing industries. It is often argued that an independent Scotland could emulate the success of Iceland and Norway in defending the sustainability of their fisheries from EU pressure. But the two Nordic countries have defended their fisheries from outside the EU. Indeed, a principal reason that they have declined so far to join the EU is that they see their fishing communities not just as a key economic asset but as an important part of their identity and culture. If Scots attached comparable value to their fishing communities, then presumably the SNP strategy for Scottish independence would not be so dependent on securing automatic EU membership as a successor state to the UK. Given that ambition, Scotland would have to find a way of securing an exemption from the *acquis communitaire* as a condition of membership – which is well nigh impossible, except as a transitional arrangement – or place its hopes for negotiating a subsequent reform of the Common Fisheries Policy on the EU's notoriously complex negotiating system of multilateral trade-offs.

Green Potential

The strongest environmental argument for independence is that to develop her natural potential for green technologies fully, Scotland needs the complete spectrum of powers available to independent states. The most obvious illustration is the need for borrowing powers. Huge investment is needed to develop the alternative technologies and the returns are not only long-term but crucially dependent on high global energy prices. One estimate is that developing Scotland's share of the UK's 'practical resource' for offshore energy will cost over £40bn to 2050. While the bulk of the capital is expected to come from commercial investors, a significant contribution from the state will be essential if Scotland is to attract a large share of the associated jobs. As a devolved part of the UK, the Scottish Government's capacity to borrow is determined by the London Treasury, which may or may not share Scottish judgements and priorities. Even if it did, in response to the crisis in the UK's public finances the Coalition Government has decreed a 36% cut in Scotland's capital spending budget over the next public spending round (Scottish Government, 2010).[7] As a devolved authority, the Scottish Government has had to spend its time hassling the UK Government for modest concessions such as the release of Scotland's £200m Fossil Fuel Levy fund, partially achieved in 2011, and in negotiating access to the EU's energy programmes and development funding options through the Whitehall bureaucracy.

By contrast, an independent Scotland would be able to back its own judgement of the development potential of its alternative energy resources and, within the limits of whatever currency union she might be a member of or the tolerance of international capital markets, to determine its own borrowing limits. Its international credit rating, meantime, would be bolstered by its continuing role as a significant oil producer and owner of substantial oil reserves as well as by its anticipated future role as an exporter of green energy in an era of rising world energy prices.

Scotland's recent history offers support for the argument that independence could progress Scotland's environmental improvement. It was a frequent claim by the SNP in the 1970s and '80s that a share of the vast revenues generated from the North Sea should be invested in the development of alternative energy technologies. Their pleas were ignored by London, allowing other countries, notably Denmark and Germany, to establish a decisive lead in the development of the first wind-powered generation of renewables. As a small, independent country, Scotland could have been expected to have been more sensitive than the UK not only to the extraordinary good fortune of its oil discoveries but also to their limited lifespan and the consequent need to use them as a legacy.

Sometimes environmental objectives clash with one another. Some environmental organisations oppose the continued proliferation of wind farms in Scotland and many communities oppose the upgrading of the Beauly–Denny overhead powerline designed to bring the future output of renewable energy in the north of Scotland to markets in the south. The reported £1bn cost of burying the power line underground or rerouting it as a subsea cable was dismissed as too expensive by the power companies as well as being beyond the capacity of the Scottish Government's capital budget. The consequence is that in approving the Beauly–Denny overland line, the Scottish Government had to sacrifice one important goal, the preservation of Scotland's natural environment along with the economic benefits of the tourism it attracts, to the even more compelling goal of reducing Scotland's carbon footprint and securing the jobs that renewables have the potential to create. If Scotland had been an independent state in ownership of the oil revenues from the Scottish sector of the North Sea, she would, on reasonable assumptions about her use of the revenues in years of surplus, have had the option of wholly or partially subsidising the alternatives to the overland option. What better use for the oil revenues than to reconcile two such fundamental goals – maximising Scotland's contribution to low carbon energy and conserving her environment?

Nuclear Risk

Independence would bring the probability of a more specific environmental benefit. As discussed in my 'International Case' for independence, an independent Scotland could be expected to insist on the removal of the Royal Navy's nuclear missile force from Faslane along with the nuclear weapons storage facility at Coulport. This would reduce the risk of Scotland's environment being exposed to the catastrophic damage caused by a major nuclear accident or by a deliberate attack by terrorists.

However we have seen that the UK Government has a policy of concentrating its entire fleet of nuclear powered submarines at Faslane, with its seven planned Astute-class hunter submarines in the process of joining the existing Trafalgar submarines and the Vanguard strategic missile submarines. It is not clear whether the rUK Government would have any interest in retaining Faslane as a submarine base following the expulsion of the nuclear missile carrying submarines. If it had, the Scottish Government's acquiescence to date in the MoD's decision to concentrate her non-nuclear weapon submarine fleet in Scotland suggests that it might have no objection. In this case, while the minimal risk of direct nuclear attack would be reduced, the continued presence of the Astute and Trafalgar nuclear-powered submarines with highly destructive conventional weapons, including Cruise missiles, which could be used in support of land forces would perpetuate the risks of terrorist attack, nuclear accidents and lower level environmental damage. The SNP Government's position on the basing of nuclear powered submarines in Scotland beyond independence needs to be clarified in the light of SNP's traditional commitment to a non-nuclear Scotland civil and military.

It is clear then, that independence could be expected to bring substantial environmental benefits in two areas – the reduction, if not complete elimination of the greatest discrete non-carbon threat to Scotland's environment, and the eventual replacement of Scotland's current fossil-based energy production by renewables.

However, on other fronts of the campaign against global warming, independence would make less difference than environmentalists would like. An independent Scotland would be unlikely to accede to the demands of the radical environmentalists for an end to the exploration for new oil reserves in the deep waters of the North Atlantic west of Shetland. Not that the environmentalists' challenge to the oil producing countries is not a serious one. George Monbiot has pointed out that if we burn just 60% of global fossil fuel reserves (as known in 2010) we will add two degrees to global warming (Monbiot, 2010).[8] But it is a safe prediction that an independent Scotland like other oil producing countries with still untested oil prospects, including the UK and Norway, would be unimpressed. Oil will almost certainly increase in value as energy demand from the industrialising developing countries grows and few countries will reject the promise of the greater wealth it offers.

Scotland would have particular reasons for pursuing the remaining opportunities. Oil would be proportionately more important to the smaller Scottish economy than to the UK economy and a Scottish Government would be under pressure in the final decades of oil to make up as far as possible for the £270bn or more of revenues surrendered to UK control in the first four decades of production. Perhaps the best that environmentalists can expect is that an independent Scotland would insist on progressively more stringent environmental safeguards for deepwater oil exploration and production and that it would follow Norway's example in being a generous financial supporter of international environmental initiatives such as the 'in trust' purchase of such global environmental commons as the Amazonian rain forests.

That would, of course, leave Scotland open to the same charge of environmental hypocrisy as Norway (Curtis, 2009).[9] Although, thanks to hydro power, Norway meets 60% of her total energy needs from renewables, her role as a major producer of fossil fuels and her high level of general consumption, means that she has the 10th highest carbon footprint in the world, equal with the UK, Germany and Denmark. With just 0.1% of the world's population, Norway is responsible for 0.3% of global greenhouse gas emissions rising to around 2% when the carbon content of her oil exports are included (Norwegian University of Science and Technology, 2010).[10] Reflecting Scotland's lower living standards Scotland's greenhouse gas emissions are estimated at 0.15% of the global total (Audit Scotland, 2011).[11] Figures for the carbon contribution of Scottish fossil fuel production are not available but it would be surprising if it did not at least double the Scottish contribution to global emissions. Scotland is also a net importer of carbon pollution through her trade deficit in manufactured goods. One estimate is that her carbon imports increased between 1995 and 2004 from 11.6m tonnes to 28m tonnes (Stockholm Environment Policy Institute, 2009).[12] The Scottish Government has estimated that such imports could be equivalent to 29% of all Scottish emissions (Scottish Government, 2010).[13]

Some champions of independence may take comfort in the probability that even with Scotland meeting only half the share of her total energy needs from renewables that Norway achieves – 30% against 60% – Scotland probably still has a lower conventional carbon footprint than Norway. But the fact is that her contribution remains at least twice the global average in a world in which carbon emissions have increased by 50% over the last two decades – and by 5.9% in 2010, even in the midst of global economic uncertainty – to reach the highest concentration of CO_2 in the atmosphere for at least 800,000 years (Global Carbon Project, 2010).[14]

Conclusion

For all the claims that Scotland has established herself as a world leader in the fight against global warming, independence would not allow Scotland to escape from the moral dilemmas of her expedient response to the climate change any more than it has allowed Norway to. The challenge to her economic ambitions and to her lifestyle would remain. But independence would yield some significant benefits. While the production of renewable energy is not the only element of a serious strategy against global warming, it is a vitally important one. Energy production remains the largest single source of Scottish emissions, at 30% of the total. In a world facing environmental catastrophe, a country which has such outstanding competitive advantages in renewables production has a moral obligation to exploit them. Scotland's direct individual contribution to the reduction of global carbon emissions reduction will always be marginal but by developing alternative technologies to exploit her natural advantages she can add to the non-carbon options available to a world in desperate need of alternatives to the fossil fuels which will dominate global production for decades to come. An independent Scotland would have the freedom to make her own judgement on what priority to give to the infrastructure of production – for example, through additional borrowing to continue with the development of Carbon Capture and Storage (CCS), which has stalled in Scotland due to the lack of consistent support from the UK Government. It would also give her the right to champion by voice and vote in international forums her own judgement of the challenges presented by global warming and the strategies needed to combat them. Not least, independence could dramatically reduce the main non-carbon challenge to Scotland's environment by expelling nuclear-powered submarines and their nuclear weapons from Scotland's land and coastal waters.

References

1   Harvie, C, *Fool's Gold: The Story of North Sea Oil*. London, 1994.

2   *Towards A Low Carbon Economy in Scotland*. Scottish Government, Edinburgh, 2010.

3   Climate Change Scotland Act 2009, Scottish Parliament, 2009.

4   *Scottish Energy 2020*. Institution of Mechanical Engineers, London, 2011.

5   Citibank *An Independent Scotland? Stranded Asset Risk for Utility and Renewable Investors*. London, 2011, reported for the Labour Party by Tom Greatrex MP.

6 Mackay, D, 'What Does Home Rule Mean for Economic Policy?' in Mackay, D (ed), *Scotland's Economic Future.* Reform Scotland, Edinburgh, 2011.

7 *Independent Budget Review.* Scottish Government, Edinburgh, 2010.

8 Monbiot, G, *The Guardian*, 28/01/2010.

9 Curtis, M, *Norway's Dirty Little Secret.* Guardiancomment 24/09/2010.

10 *International Carbon Emissions 2010.* Norwegian University of Science and Technology, Oslo, 2010.

11 *Reducing Scotland's Greenhouse Gas Emissions.* Auditor General for Scotland, 2011.

12 *The Need for Good Carbon Accounting in Scotland.* Stockholm Environment Policy Institute. University of York, 2009.

13 Scottish Government Carbon Assessment Project: Phase 2 Report, *2010–14 Annual Emission Survey.* Global Carbon Project, 2011.

14 Global Carbon Project, *Annual Emission Survey,* 2010.

'Aye but...'

'Aye, but...'

SOME WILL REMAIN UNPERSUADED that the case has been made for Scottish independence. Others, while being attracted to the overall case, will harbour specific doubts. Here I have set out concise responses to some of the most common expressions of 'Aye, but...'

As a small country in an uncertain world would Scotland be able to maintain the same AAA credit rating that the UK has maintained in the financial crisis so far?

There can be no guarantee that an independent Scotland would be given a triple-A rating by the ratings agencies, but her prospects would be good. Currently an independent Scotland's debt/GDP rating, including North Sea oil, would be around 56%, comfortably below the traditional 60% level for a triple-A rating.

However, the global crisis has overthrown traditional standards and Scotland may well face a legacy of national debt from the UK well above 60% of her GDP. On the other hand, Scotland has substantial collateral in her North Sea oil reserves and would, presumably, not have the handicap of being a member of the eurozone. Scotland's Nordic neighbours – even Finland, as a member of the eurozone – all enjoy triple ratings, as do the Netherlands within the eurozone and Switzerland outwith it. It's worth remembering that credit ratings are no more than recommendations by commercial ratings companies and that lenders make their own decisions on the rates they charge on loans to governments.

Surely the rest of the UK (rUK) would wash its hands of an independent Scotland, leaving its citizens to face the risks and uncertainties of global politics on our own?

The rUK would no longer have any official responsibility for Scotland but it would share not only 300 years and more of mutual, if sometimes fractious, history but also important common interests. These would include trade and investment, the need to maintain the security of the British Isles, the operation of a common UK labour market, an interest in coordinating English and Scottish positions in international bodies such as the UN and regional structures such as the EU where that was feasible, collaboration in scientific research and cultural affairs, possibly a common currency agreement, and arrangements for a shared monarchy and membership of the Commonwealth. An intergovernmental and parliamentary Council of our entire archipelago, perhaps, like the Nordic Council, would be one possible model for continued cooperation.

But, yes, we would depend on our own decisions and will for success in a way that we haven't done for 300 years.

Is Scotland not heading towards a more authoritarian society? Following the SNP's success in the Scottish elections of May 2011 the party is using the overall parliamentary majority it achieved to manipulate the Parliament for its own party purposes. The SNP's insistence on providing the Parliament's Presiding Officer as well as a majority of the committee chairs is one sign that Scotland is on an authoritarian curve. The SNP Government's introduction of laws against sectarian singing and chanting at football matches is another.

It is not unusual in parliamentary systems that a party winning an overall majority should use that majority to ensure the delivery of the election pledges on which it was elected. The real test of parliamentary democracy is whether the majority party attempts to limit the minority parties' opportunities to challenge the Government. There is no sign of that happening. The new anti-sectarian law has its supporters and critics across the political spectrum. Like laws against racism, it does involve a limitation on absolute freedom of speech but in the interests of preventing public disorder and violence.

Under independence would Scots still be able to enjoy their favourite BBC *and* ITV *programmes?*

Yes. An agreement would be reached between a Scottish Broadcasting Authority and UK broadcasters to ensure that Scottish viewers and listeners would be able to access their favourite BBC programmes alongside an increased output of Scottish produced news, sports and drama programmes. What price a Scottish equivalent of the Danish *Borgen* or *The Killing*?

Scots don't have the confidence to manage their own affairs. Remember the Darien disaster of 1700 when up to 50% of Scotland's capital was lost in a vainglorious attempt to compete with England in building a Scottish trading empire based in Panama. Better to depend on the superior experience and wealth of Britain than risk going it ourselves again.

Times have changed. A world-wide system of free trade has replaced the exclusive trading systems fashionable in the 17th and 18th centuries and Great Britain's economic power and political prestige have waned dramatically since its imperial heyday. Among the world's developed economies the UK has the highest level after Japan of overall debt (public and private); its economy is seriously unbalanced between services and manufacturing as well as between regions of the country; and its class-ridden institutions of Government seem incapable of reform. The best models for Scotland's future are the small welfare state democracies of western Europe. Meanwhile Scotland's experience of devolution, particularly the last five years with SNP Government, has shown that Scots can govern with competence and ambition.

As part of the UK we share the costs of running government with the other 60m UK citizens. How could we afford the extra costs of running Scotland as a separate state?

Under devolution, Scotland already meets many of the costs of government. Independence would add some extra costs – for example, in administering our own tax system – but it would also offer new opportunities to save money, from the £670m a year that Scotland contributes to the UK's 'external services' and the several £millions it contributes each year towards the costs of the UK's nuclear deterrent to the smaller sums it would save by not having to pay for the House of Lords or London-based events such as the London 2012 Olympics. Other developed democracies of similar size to Scotland, such as Norway and Finland, represent their own interests and values in international affairs and think of the costs as a valuable investment in their future.

If the uncertainty over the future of the eurozone makes membership of the single currency unattractive for the foreseeable future doesn't that mean that Scotland would be forced to stick with sterling? In which case, what would be the point of independence?

Countries choose their currency arangements for motives of pragmatism and prestige. As a small country, Scotland would be likely to focus on the pragmatic. If membership of the eurozone is excluded for the time being the immediate choice would be between a separate Scottish currency like the Norwegian or Swedish kroner, membership of a sterling zone, or some managed relationship with sterling.

Each of the options carries its own balance of advantages and disadvantages. Moving straight to a separate Scottish currency would be risky, especially while the European fiscal crisis remains unresolved. That leaves full membership of sterling or a Scottish pound pegged to sterling as the Danish kroner is pegged to the euro. Both options would leave Westminster in control of the currency though the second would leave some scope for interest rate variations. That would put the onus of running a separate economic policy on fiscal policy within the budgetary parameters set by the senior currency partner. Scotland's recent fiscal record suggests that with control of her own tax base and the full range of spending decisions Scotland's prospects of running budgets within the probable deficit limits are more favourable than those of the rUK. But as for any country the successful management of the economy within the limits set by formal commitments and the global financial markets would be a major challenge.

After all we've shared – empire, innumerable wars, economic crises, the creation of the NHS and the welfare state – isn't it somehow disloyal of us to go our own way?

We've shared a lot – some of it good, some of it bad – but as the smaller partner we're the ones who've usually had to adapt to English preferences. Think of the all the years we've spent living under Westminster Governments which have never won a majority in Scotland: 2012 is the 30th in the 62 years since the Second World War in which Scots have been governed by Westminster Governments they have rejected at the polls. In their steady rightward trend, the Governments we've rejected have arguably been progressively more hostile to Scotland's political preferences. Think what Thatcher and now the Cameron-Clegg coalition are doing to the welfare state and to the NHS in England. Perhaps it's the English political establishment which is being disloyal to the Scottish majority, not the Scottish majority which is being disloyal to England.

There seem to be plenty of experts lining up to warn of the elephant traps waiting for an independent Scotland – the size of the national debt, the costs of getting rid of Trident, the uncertainty over Scotland being admitted to the EU, how if we do we'll have to join the eurozone. They can't all be wrong can they?

Experts come in many forms. Some use their expertise as a smokescreen for their political opinions. Others, particularly academics, often couch their contributions to the debate in terms of a possibility of such and such happening only to have the press present their views as being much more categorical than they really are. Usually it's not long before other commentators come forward with counter examples and more nuanced views. When the topic is the EU, remember that the EU and its treaties are a playground for lawyers. If the EU had followed the letter of its own laws it would look very different today – and might not even exist.

The EU is fundamentally a political project and regularly discounts its laws and regulations against its political interests. The rUK and the EU will both have a strong interest in cooperating with Scotland and, after some huffing and puffing, they will follow that interest.

By claiming our independence, can you be sure that we're not going to provoke a wave of nationalist extremism on both sides of the border?

A large and growing proportion of English voters appear to favour Scottish independence, some because they believe that they subsidise the Scots, some because they believe that devolution gives Scots MPs a privileged position at Westminster (which it does) and some because they simply see us a nuisance. Yet others favour it because they believe that it would force the English to consider more radical reforms of their own public institutions and electoral systems. UK political leaders of all parties have accepted that if a majority of Scots want independence Westminster would have no grounds for refusing it. There may be a few ultra English patriots who would consider making trouble but the great majority in the two countries would expect their Governments to work out a new relationship between the two countries which would ensure that the two economies could continue to trade and invest with the minimum of disruption.

Could there be a worse time for Scotland to go independent than the worst global economic crisis for 60 years?

It would certainly be better if the global prospect was for steady economic growth on the back of currency stability and a balanced world economy. But if the case for independence is well founded it will be good for the worst of times as for the best of times. Being part of a UK in long-term economic decline and with chronic fiscal and trading imbalances – symptoms of that decline gives us no protection against the global crisis. The question in bad times or good times is: are we likely to be better off taking our own decisions than allowing others to take decisions over our heads?

Our population is too old, too sick and too dependent on the state to allow Scotland to flourish as an independent country.

Scotland does have serious social problems which present significant economic challenges, among them high levels of ill health and an ageing population which will increase the dependency rate (the ratio of the non-working population to the working population). The problems are concentrated in the poorer 15–20% of the population and are particularly acute in Glasgow and other parts of the west of Scotland. There are no simple or quick solutions, but independence would provide the opportunities for fresh responses. For example, it would allow Scotland to pursue its own policy to attract new immigrants, to integrate health and social care expenditure with benefits policy and to pursue its own labour market policies.

In expenditure terms, Scotland spends a little more proportionately on social protection than the UK overall – 9.1% of the UK total on a population share of 8.4% – but these higher costs are included in the official annual ONS/Scottish Government GERS figures, which show Scotland in recent years in a stronger fiscal position than the UK as whole. But by any measure, this will be one of the major challenges an independent Scotland will face.

We Scots have been here before haven't we, talking up our glittering prospects – It's Scotland's Oil, Argentina 1978, the 1979 Assembly referendum, Silicon Glen – why should it be different this time?

Well, throw in Darien, Culloden, Mrs Thatcher and Ravenscraig why don't you? For those of us of a certain age, the old disappointments will always be raw. But there's a new generation, more than one, which knows little of these old frustrations. Their memories are more likely to be of Tony Blair and Iraq, Gordon Brown and the financial crisis, David Cameron and Nick Clegg cutting left, right and centre – and of Alex

Salmond offering a more positive vision of Scotland's future at the head of a competent SNP Government and a professional administration. Hubris will always shadow ambition, but rather ambition with the risk of hubris than no ambition at all.

Surely the experience of Ireland and Iceland shows that it is too risky for small countries to go it alone?

What Ireland and Iceland show is that small countries are no more immune to major errors of policy than large countries. Italy and Spain are facing difficulties hardly less serious than those facing Ireland and Iceland and the UK does not lack its problems either. At the beginning of 2012, Iceland, and to lesser extent Ireland, appear to be taking the first steps towards recovery while Spain, Italy and the UK are still struggling to stabilise. Perhaps small countries have more flexibility to correct their errors than larger countries. Most of the small established democracies of western Europe – the Netherlands, Finland, Norway, Switzerland, Denmark and Sweden – have come through the crisis so far in better shape than many larger countries. Risk is ever-present for both small and large, but it can be minimised by good government.

Will we have to give up the monarchy – that's one bit of the old country I would miss.

Like the population as a whole, supporters of independence embrace a mix of views on the monarchy. The SNP's position is that Scotland should retain the monarchy after independence.

Independence is really just one man's obsession isn't it? Without Salmond there would be no SNP Government and no independence referendum either.

Alex Salmond is certainly the central figure in the independence movement and crucial to its success. But he is standing on the shoulders of several generations of previous campaigners, over 20,000 current

SNP members and at least a third of Scottish voters of all parties and none who believe Scotland should be independent. And in addition to the many prominent Scots from all walks of life who support independence, the SNP Government contains other personalities such as Nicola Sturgeon, John Swinney, Kenny MacAskill and Mike Russell who have proved themselves substantial politicians in their own right.

Presumably I would have to carry a Scottish passport as a citizen of an independent Scotland. That wouldn't carry as much clout as a UK passport, would it?

The exact nature of the passport carried by Scottish citizens will be determined by Scotland's relationship with the EU. Assuming membership, the passport would be an EU passport with a Scottish identification. If Scotland does not immediately become a member of the EU, then a transitional arrangement to continue using UK passports would probably be made while Scotland established her own consular services, probably in cooperation with other countries. The process of Scotland becoming independent would generate enormous publicity around the world and Scotland could expect her international clout to be comparable to that of the Nordic countries, with less diplomatic muscle than the UK, but perhaps more international goodwill.

Under independence, would I have a guarantee that my state and public sector pensions would continue to be paid at the same level as I would be entitled to as part of the UK?

The future of pensions is a matter of debate and controversy throughout the UK. The value of the state pension is more secure at the moment than the future of public sector occupational pensions, which are subject both to increases in employees' and employers' contributions and reductions in future pay-outs. It is probable that the value of state pensions in an independent Scotland would be guaranteed for a period after independence, but the size of the state pensions bill for Scotland, around £7bn in 2009–10, means that it could not be guaranteed indefinitely any more than it is within the UK. However the growth of pensioners as a proportion of the Scottish population means that they are well placed politically to defend the value of their pensions.

I have got family and friends in England. Would I find myself cut off from them after independence or subject to border checks each time I wanted to visit?

No. It would be in the interests of both Scotland and the rest of the UK that movement between the different former parts of the UK should be free as it is currently between Ireland and the UK. At most you might be expected to carry some form of identification when visiting England. If Scotland pursued a different immigration policy from the rUK the numbers involved would be so small compared to immigration into the rUK that we could expect the two countries to find a system of internal checks sufficient.

Alistair Darling has warned that the 'downsides [of independence] are immense, the risks amazing.' As a former Chancellor he should know, shouldn't he?

And yet in the same interview (*The Observer*, 15 January 2012) Darling was clear that Scotland could go it alone and that his starting point was 'What is best for Scotland?', a rather less apocalyptic position. His argument is that an independent Scotland would have no satisfactory currency option. Entry to the eurozone is ruled out because under the pressure of the current crisis the eurozone is likely to move towards a tighter fiscal union while a separate Scottish currency is ruled out because of the risks of launching a new currency at time of global uncertainty. Which leaves some arrangement with sterling. Darling presents this as if the only alternative was a full currency union with tight tax, spend and deficit rules imposed by Westminster equivalent to economic if not political union. But to function a currency union requires only effective deficit rules: if its members observe the deficit rules then it does not matter what level of tax and spending they operate at; high tax and high spend or low tax and low spend. The crisis in the eurozone arose because many of its members, including some of its biggest, failed to observe their own rules on deficits and debt ratios. The probability is that an independent Scotland would be able to meet the debt and deficit rules of a sterling currency union while still enjoying a critical measure of discretion to pursue tax and spend policies more sympathetic to its economic needs than available under economic and political union.

But a full currency union is not the only possible arrangement involving sterling. Scotland could unilaterally peg its currency to sterling without accepting any formal deficit rules, let alone tax and spend rules, using instead the full range of levers including interest rates to maintain the parity.

Darling invokes the risks of independence. He ignores the risks to Scotland of remaining in the Union. The risk, for example, of being governed from London by parties persistently rejected by Scottish voters and hostile to Scottish policy preferences. The risk that the remaining 40% of Scotland's oil wealth will follow the 60% that has already been creamed off by London with only a Barnett 9–10% returned to Scotland. The risks attached to Scotland's conscription as the UK's sole nuclear weapons base. The risk that UK monetary policy, not to mention its policy on financial regulation, will continue to be set by the interests of the City of London. It's not only change that involves risk: the status quo carries its share too.

Scotland is too divided internally to be able to make a go of independence. Think of the religious sectarianism, the rising number of recorded incidents of racism, the Glasgow–Edinburgh rivalry, even antagonism between Scots and English people living in Scotland...

Even though the majority of Scots probably never experience let alone practice sectarianism, it is a serious problem which has rightly commanded the attention of successive governments. Though the current government has introduced new legislation directed specifically at sectarianism connected to football the overall solutions are much wider – economic and social change improving the life prospects of the most susceptible communities, further publicity and education for young people and the closer social integration of Catholic and non-Catholic schools. It is worrying that despite less than 2% of Scotland's population being of Afro-Caribbean or Asian origin, the number of recorded incidents of racism continues to grow at a significant rate, though the figures include a surprising number of white British victims of racism by other white people of various identities. The Glasgow–Edinburgh rivalry is of a different order and as much about economic and cultural competition and politics as about identity. But Scotland is not alone in having such problems. England has more serious problems of racism, as do countries like the Netherlands, the Nordic countries and Germany and France which have higher immigrant populations than Scotland. There is nothing in the record of the many other countries which experience similar problems to suggest that Scotland's problems of sectarianism and racism would disable her as an independent country.

Many of the good things about the Union – the welfare state, the NHS, for example – were built after the Second World War by the combined efforts and taxes of English, Scots, Welsh and Irish people together. By going independent and withdrawing Scottish MPs from Westminster, would we Scots not be handing political power at Westminster to those Tory (and Labour politicians) who have little regard for the founding vision behind the NHS and the welfare state?

The loss of Scottish MPs from Westminster would certainly make it easier for the Tories to win elections in the rUK. But this change is the result of two developments – a long-term trend in the political choices of English voters in the south-east and less consistently in the Midlands away from Labour towards the Tories and a loss of faith in social democracy within the Labour Party.

By contrast, in Scotland the two leading parties, SNP and Labour, have remained more loyal to traditional social democracy. That is what secured the majorities in the Scottish Parliament for free social care, an integrated NHS and no university tuition fees. We know that the retention of Scottish MPs at Westminster cannot guarantee majorities there for social democracy.

So should Scotland continue sacrificing its own interests and political values to the preferences of English voters? And for how much longer?

In reality, it is improbable that English voters would accept perpetual Tory rule. It seems unlikely that there is a natural English majority for the policies pursued by an increasingly brazen free-market Tory party dominated by the City of London. By facing English voters with the reality that they could no longer rely on Scottish votes for periodic relief from right-wing Governments, Scottish independence could prompt a realignment of English politics creating a centre-left majority of progressive Labour, Liberal Democrats and Greens committed to challenging the sources of inertia in English public life – the first-past-the-post voting system, the dominance of the City and of English public schools and Oxbridge, the centralisation of power in London, the obsession with Britain's great power status and its expensive accoutrements such as the nuclear deterrent. By demonstrating that there are different ways of organising society and of being a useful member of the international community, an independent Scotland could make its own modest contribution to that realignment.

Select Bibliography

Books from the last three decades arguing for independence:

Scott, Paul Henderson (ed), *A Nation Again: Why Independence Will be Good for Scotland (and England too)*. Luath Press, Edinburgh, 2011.

Reid, Harry and Scott, Paul Henderson (eds), *The Independence Book: Scotland in Today's World*. Luath Press, Edinburgh, 2008.

Brown, R, (ed), *Nation In A State: Independent Perspectives on Scottish Independence*. Ten Books Press, Dunfermline, 2007.

Scott, Paul Henderson, *Still In Bed with the Elephant*. Saltire Society, Edinburgh, 1988.

Gray, Alasdair, *Why Scots Should Rule Scotland*. Canongate, Edinburgh, 1992.

Russell, Michael and Macleod, Dennis, *Grasping the Thistle*. Argyll Publishing, Argyll 2006.

MacAskill, Kenny, *Building A Nation: Post-Devolution Nationalism in Scotland*. Luath Press, Edinburgh, 2004.

Sillars, Jim, *Scotland: the Case for Optimism*. Polygon, Edinburgh, 1986.

Books exploring some of the key issues for the independence case in a 'post-sovereign' world:

MacCormick, Neil, *Questioning Sovereignty*. Oxford University Press, 1999.

Keating, Michael, *The Independence of Scotland*. Oxford University Press, 2009.

Paterson, Lindsay, *The Autonomy of Modern Scotland*. Edinburgh University Press, 2004.

List of Acronyms

BIS   Bank for International Settlements

ECAS   Edinburgh Cripple Aid Society

EEA   European Economic Area

EFTA   European Free Trade Association

EU   European Union

FFA   full fiscal autonomy

GDP   Gross Domestic Product

GERS   Government Expenditure and Revenue in Scotland

IAEA   International Atomic Energy Agency

ICC   International Criminal Court

ITU   International Telecommunications Union

MSP   Member of the Scottish Parliament

NATO   North Atlantic Treaty Organisation

NSD   Norwegian Social Science Data Services

OECD   Organisation for Economic Cooperation and Development

PFI   Private Finance Initiative

PPI   Producer Price Index

rUK   rest of the United Kingdom

SEAD   Scottish Education and Action for Development

SCVO   Scottish Council for Voluntary Organisations

UN   United Nations

USSR   Union of Soviet Socialist Republics

VTT   Valtion Teknillinen Tutkimuskeskus

WTO   World Trade Organisation

Some other books published by Luath Press

The Case for Left Wing Nationalism
Stephen Maxwell
ISBN: 978 1 908373 8 8 PBK £9.99

Blossom: What Scotland Needs to Flourish
Lesley Riddoch
ISBN: 978 1 908373 69 4 PBK £11.99

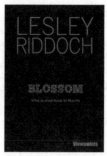

Spanning four politically and socially tumultuous decades, Stephen Maxwell's essays explore the origins and development of the Scottish Nationalist movement. As an instrumental member of the SNP, lifelong activist and intellectual, Maxwell provides a unique insight into the debate over Scottish independence.

The Case for Left Wing Nationalism considers the class dynamics of the constitutional debate, deconstructs the myths that underpin Scottish political culture and exposes the role Scottish institutions have played in restricting Scotland's progress.

In this wide-ranging analysis, Maxwell draws on a wealth of cultural, economic and historical sources.

From debating the very nature of nationalism itself, to tackling the immediate social issues that Scotland faces, Maxwell establishes a very real picture of contemporary Scotland and its future.

To succeed, Left Wing Nationalism must look to Scotland's future not her past. It could do worse than adopt as its slogan Hugh MacDairmid's prescription for a Scottish renaissance: 'Not traditions – precedents!' STEPHEN MAXWELL

Weeding out vital components of Scottish identity from decades of political and social tangle is no mean task, but it's one journalist Lesley Riddoch has undertaken.

Dispensing with the tired, yo-yoing jousts over fiscal commissions, Devo Something and EU in-or-out, *Blossom* pinpoints both the buds of growth and the blight that's holding Scotland back. Drawing from its people and history, as well as the experience of the Nordic countries and the author's own passionate and outspoken perspective, this is a plain-speaking but incisive call to restore equality and control to local communities and let Scotland flourish.

**A Model Constitution for Scotland:
Making Democracy Work in an
Independent Scotland**
W. Elliot Bulmer
ISBN 978 1 908373 13 7 PBK £9.99

**A Nation Again: Why Independence will
be good for Scotland (and England too)**
With a Foreword by Alec Salmond
Edited by Paul Henderson Scott
ISBN 978 1906817 67 1 PBK £7.99

*Scotland is a free, sovereign and
independent commonwealth. Its form
of government is a parliamentary
democracy based upon the sovereignty of
the people, social justice, solidarity and
respect for human rights...*

A Model Constitution for Scotland
sets out a workable model for
Scotland's future and includes detailed
constitutional proposals together with
informed discussion on the topic.

*The independence debate has to break
out of political elites and address
the 'after independence' question.
Elliot Bulmer's book is an important
contribution to this, exploring how we
make Scotland constitutionally literate,
and how we shape our politics in a way
which reflects who we are and what we
aspire to be. Bulmer rightly argues that
independence has to aspire to more than
abolishing reserved powers, Holyrood
becoming a mini-Westminster, and
nothing else changing. A must read for
independentistas, thoughtful unionists
and democrats.* GERRY HASSAN, author
and broadcaster

*Bulmer deals with fundamental rights
and freedoms in a broad-minded and
incisive fashion.* NEWSNET SCOTLAND

*If you believe in the Case for
Independence, this book will provide
you with a stirring endorsement of your
view. If you are sceptical, it might well
persuade you to convert to the cause.
If you are downright hostile, this book
could be dangerous – it could prompt
you to rethink.*

Suddenly Scottish Independence is within
grasp. Is this a frivolous pipe dream, a
romantic illusion? Or is it, as the writers
of this dynamic and positive collection
of essays insist, an authentic political
option, feasible and beneficial?

As the Scottish people prepare for their
biggest ever collective decision, this
book forcefully sets out the Case for
Independence. The distinguished authors,
from a variety of different perspectives,
argue the case for the Imperative of
Independence.

Radical Scotland: Arguments for Self-Determination
Edited by Gerry Hassan and Rosie Ilett
ISBN 978 1906817 94 7 PBK £12.99

Building a Nation: Post Devolution Nationalism in Scotland
Kenny MacAskill
ISBN 978 1842820 81 0 PBK £4.99

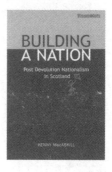

Scotland believes it is a radical, egalitarian, inclusive nation. It was hoped that the establishment of the Scottish Parliament was going to give expression to this. Instead, we have witnessed a minimal, unattractive politics with little to choose between the main parties. This might be adequate in the good times, but no more. *Radical Scotland* explores how we can go beyond the limited politics we have experienced and makes the case for shifting from self-government politically to self-determination as a society and a nation. It asks how do we shake up institutional Scotland? How do we shift power and give people voice?

The editors Gerry Hassan and Rosie Ilett have brought together in one volume some of the most original thinkers in our nation making the case for a very different politics and society. It includes conversations with leading global figures on some of the key issues facing the world which impact on Scotland.

Where stands Scotland post Devolution and what is the future for Nationalism in a devolved Parliament? Is the Scottish Parliament a Unionist dead end or a Nationalist highway to Independence? Has Devolution killed the SNP stone dead or given it a platform to build from? These are questions that need to be answered as Scotland begins to come to terms with Devolution and decides where to go next.

In this book, Kenny MacAskill searches for the answers to these questions, which are vital to the future of Scotland. He makes the case for a distinctive Scottish version of social democracy that can balance a vibrant economy with quality public services, and believes that Post Devolution Nationalism is about Building a Nation to be proud of.

A manifesto to inspire and infuriate; pacey, intelligent and accessible. Like all good political pamphlets it is best enjoyed when read out loud.
SCOTTISH REVIEW OF BOOKS

Agenda for a New Scotland: Visions of Scotland 2020

Kenny MacAskill

ISBN 978 1905222 00 1 PBK £9.99

Scotland: Land and Power: Agenda for Land Reform

Andy Wightman

ISBN 978 0946487 70 7 PBK £5.00

The campaign for a Scottish Parliament was ongoing for centuries. Lamented in prose and championed in print. Petitioned for, marched in support of and voted upon. Dear to the hearts of many and whose absence broke the hearts of a few. From Kenny MacAskill's Introduction to *Agenda for a New Scotland*.

It has now reconvened after nearly 300 years. A Devolved Legislature but a Parliament all the same. Unable to address all issues but able to make a difference in many areas. It is for the Scottish Parliament to shape and mould the future of Scotland. But, what should that future be?

This is a series of contributed articles from politicians, academics and Civic Scotland. They outline opportunities and future directions for Scotland across a range of areas socially, economically and politically. This is an *Agenda for a New Scotland*. Visions of what Scotland can be by 2020.

Land reform campaigner Andy Wightman delivers a hard-hitting critique of the oppressive absurdities of Scotland's antiquated land laws. His is by no means a purely negative analysis – here are thought-through proposals for reforms which he argues would free both country and urban Scots from the shackles of land laws that are feudal and oppressive.

Andy Wightman's views are controversial, but he doesn't mind a good argument. He is an influential figure in Scottish political life these days. Those who don't agree with his views do pay attention to them, and his contribution to one of the hottest debates of the new millennium is well respected.

Writers like Andy Wightman are determined to make sure the hurt of the last century is not compounded by a rushed solution in the next. This accessible, comprehensive but passionately argued book is quite simply essential reading and perfectly timed – here's hoping Scotland's legislators agree.
LESLEY RIDDOCH

Scotland: The Growing Divide
Old Nation, New Ideas

Henry McLeish, edited by Tom Brown
ISBN 978 1908373 45 8 PBK £11.99

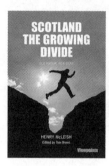

Scotlands of the Future: Sustainability
in a Small Nation

Edited by Eurig Scandrett
ISBN 978 1842820 35 3 PBK £7.99

In 2007, Scotland: The Road Divides posed a provocative political question: Had the SNP victory at Holyrood changed forever the mindset of Scottish politics?

As a Scottish Independence referendum fast approaches, Scotland: The Growing Divide returns to answer this question and more with a hard-hitting, incisive and informed look at where the devolution journey has taken us – from the heady days of the new Blair government in 1997 to the Independence referendum in 2014. It poses new questions about the issues facing Scottish politics:

How has devolution altered Scotland's national perception of itself?

Is there a fusion of identity and nationality politics with traditional politics and priorities taking place in Scotland?

Is this creating a serious realignment of political thinking and ideas?

Arguing that the Union must adapt to survive, this book maintains that many politicians have yet to come to terms with these dramatic changes and do not appear to understand the 'new politics'.

What sort of future is possible for Scotland?

How can citizens of a small nation at the periphery of the global economy make a difference?

Can Scotland's economy be sustainable? How do we build a good quality of life without damaging others'?

Scotlands of the Future looks at where we've got to, where we can go next, and where we want to get to.

This book is a contribution to building a sustainable economy in Scotland, a change that will only come about through action throughout civil society. The contributors are all working for a sustainable economy at the front line: through trade unions, business organisations, the women's movement and environmental groups, and at Scotland's parliament. They bring their experiences of transforming the real world to their vision of a transformed Scotland.
EURIG SCANDRETT, Editor

Scotland: A Suitable Case for Treatment

Tom Brown and Henry McLeish
ISBN 978 1 906307 69 1 PBK £9.99

Symptoms: the initial signs of a problem.
Diagnosis: analysis of the problem
Treatment: suggested solutions

Henry McLeish, former First Minister of Scotland and Tom Brown, one of Scotland's leading political commentators, are joined by eminent psychologist Anne Ellis as they follow on from their politically provocative *Scotland: the Road Divides* by putting Scotland on the therapist's couch. They assess what in our past has led to a present nation that is such a strange clamjamfry. Light and dark, brash but with a constant chip on its shoulder, Scotland's Jekyll and Hyde nature is shown to have led to serious social and political problems including anti-social behaviour, and borderline or real poverty.

The first part of the book asks us 'tae see ourselves as ithers see us' and the remainder deals with how Scotland should see itself. It asks the difficult question: Scotland – who are we? We ourselves are typical Scots, conscious that we have our fair share of the flaws examined in this book. Recognising our failings is the first step… We warmly encourage readers – be they policymakers or otherwise – to engage in these issues. In this complex modern world there are no easy answers. But we have to keep asking the questions.
TOM BROWN and HENRY MCLEISH

Arts of Resistance: Poets, Portraits and Landscapes of Modern Scotland

Alan Riach and Alexander Moffat, with contributions by Linda MacDonald-Lewis
ISBN 978 1 906817 18 3 PBK £16.99

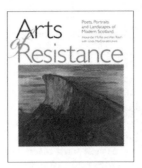

The role of art in the modern world is to challenge and provoke, to resist stagnation and to question complacency. All art, whether poetry, painting or prose, represents and interprets the world. Its purpose is to bring new perspectives to what life can be. ALEXANDER MOFFAT and ALAN RIACH

… an inspiration, a revelation and education as to the extraordinary richness and organic cohesion of twentieth-century Scottish culture, full of intellectual adventure… a landmark book. TIMES LITERARY SUPPLEMENT

Details of these and other books published by Luath Press can be found at
www.luath.co.uk

Luath Press Limited

committed to publishing well written books worth reading

LUATH PRESS takes its name from Robert Burns, whose little collie Luath (*Gael.*, swift or nimble) tripped up Jean Armour at a wedding and gave him the chance to speak to the woman who was to be his wife and the abiding love of his life. Burns called one of the 'Twa Dogs' Luath after Cuchullin's hunting dog in Ossian's *Fingal*.
Luath Press was established in 1981 in the heart of Burns country, and is now based a few steps up the road from Burns' first lodgings on Edinburgh's Royal Mile. Luath offers you distinctive writing with a hint of unexpected pleasures.
Most bookshops in the UK, the US, Canada, Australia, New Zealand and parts of Europe, either carry our books in stock or can order them for you. To order direct from us, please send a £sterling cheque, postal order, international money order or your credit card details (number, address of cardholder and expiry date) to us at the address below. Please add post and packing as follows: UK – £1.00 per delivery address; overseas surface mail – £2.50 per delivery address; overseas airmail – £3.50 for the first book to each delivery address, plus £1.00 for each additional book by airmail to the same address. If your order is a gift, we will happily enclose your card or message at no extra charge.

Luath Press Limited

543/2 Castlehill
The Royal Mile
Edinburgh EH1 2ND
Scotland
Telephone: +44 (0)131 225 4326 (24 hours)
Fax: +44 (0)131 225 4324
email: sales@luath. co.uk
Website: www. luath.co.uk